FALCON

'While presenting the falcon as a creature superbly adapted to its environment, Macdonald's scientific but lyrical study also celebrates its mythical, cultural and iconic significance.' – *The Times*

'[a] marvellous book' – *The Spectator*

'This is a wonderful book. It is not a falconry text, nor is it a falcon biology or a conservation one. Macdonald's slim volume is far more ambitious: it is an attempt to capture and indeed explain the essence of the falcon. This is simply a most beautifully considered social history of the genus *Falco* . . . it informs and provokes in equal measure . . . Macdonald writes beautifully and with a refreshing clarity.' – *The Falconer*

'accompanied by sumptious illustrations, Helen Macdonald gives us not just the natural history but the cultural history as well . . . Even for the non-ornithologist this book provides fascinating insights. Essential reading for the enthusiast.' – *The Tablet*

'What Macdonald does with *Falcon* is bring all of herself to the subject. She breathes life into the work; pulls the lives of falcons and people together into a rare three-dimensional portrait. The effect is beautiful and lasting.' – *North American Falconers Association*

'a pleasure to read . . . a trained historian of science and a passionate falconer, Macdonald's personal experience and knowledge bear fruitfully on this elegant account. The book is a must for anyone interested in animals.' – *British Journal of the History of Science*

'The book's author – the historian of science, avid falconer, and gifted writer Helen Macdonald – succeeds brilliantly . . . a smart, engaging and multidisciplinary account that vividly brings her subject to life.' – *Journal of the History of Biology*

Falcon

Helen Macdonald

reaktion books

Published by Reaktion Books Ltd
Unit 32, Waterside
44–48 Wharf Road
London N1 7UX, UK
www.reaktionbooks.co.uk

First published 2006, reprinted 2015
This edition first published 2016

Printed and bound in Great Britain by Bell & Bain, Glasgow

A catalogue record for this book is available from the British Library

ISBN 978 1 78023 641 4

Contents

Pisanello, *Young Falcon*, c. 1435, watercolour drawing.

Preface to the 2016 Edition

YOU DON'T HAVE to have read *H is for Hawk* to read this book. It works entirely on its own. But if you have, there are things in its pages you'll find familiar. The man in one photograph holding a white gyrfalcon is my dear friend Erin, who burned a Christmas tree with me on a snowy Maine lawn the winter after my father died. And you'll encounter other things you'll remember here, though they're discussed in finer detail, such as J. A. Baker, T. H. White, Nazi hawks and the opening scene of the film *A Canterbury Tale*. *Falcon* has far more in-depth discussion of the cultural history of falconry and birds of prey across thousands of years, along with musings on anatomy, physiology, hunting strategies, flight mechanics and conservation philosophy and practice. But at heart, just like *H is for Hawk*, this book is about how we use nature as a mirror. About how encounters with animals are always to some extent encounters with ourselves and with who we think we are. That unconscious trap is the one I fell into when I trained my goshawk, even after having written this book. That's how invisible and strong it is.

How did *Falcon* come about? Back in the early 2000s I was working on my doctoral dissertation at the University of Cambridge. I never finished it. I wrote this book instead. Which was surprising, because I considered myself a dedicated academic.

I loved my university department, my city; loved that every morning I could walk through tree-lined streets to one of the world's great libraries and spend the day bathed in the dusty almond and vanilla scent of aged paper, surrounded by piles of journals and books, happily checking references and taking notes on articles and texts while pigeons clattered on the roof-tiles above the desks in the North Wing.

My dissertation was on the history of science. Specifically, it was about the history of natural history and how we relate to the natural world. It was also about how we draw boundaries between things we consider to be science and things we don't. Those borders are more permeable than we generally suppose. Investigating how they are made and policed tells us a lot about the nature of science, about how we approach knowledge, and about ourselves. My lifelong obsession with birds of prey had spurred me to investigate these questions in the context of the cultures that surrounded them in the twentieth century: raptor conservation, falconry, amateur natural history and birding. I thought it would be an ideal PhD topic. It was. But, as it turned out, I wasn't an ideal PhD student.

As part of my dissertation research I spent several months in the Archives of Falconry at the World Center for Birds of Prey in Idaho. The Archives hold everything from medieval manuscript letters to modern first editions; from sealskin parkas to a stuffed goshawk once owned by Hermann Goering. As I pored over the collections, assisted with great kindness by the Archives' curator, Colonel Kent Carnie, I became more and more bewitched by the things I found. Here were obsessions, myths, fragments from distant cultures and missives from long-lost ways of life; works by people who had spent their lives in thrall to creatures they viewed in near-religious terms. Parts of me that weren't just an academic historian began to whisper that there were extraordinary things here I couldn't fit into my thesis, and that grieved me. And there was something else. Increasingly I was feeling sad that many of the elegant and thought-provoking theories and concepts I'd encountered in academia, things that helped me to understand why we see the natural world the way we do, weren't more widely known. Couldn't be, because most of us aren't granted access to the kinds of places and forums where such things are written and discussed. And that seemed very unfair to me. It still does.

Back in England, still musing on this, I had a chance meeting in the university library tearoom with Jonathan Burt, the editor of Reaktion's Animal series. He suggested that I write this book. Over coffee and a sandwich I told him I would. And I did. I wrote it for everyone, not just for historians and cultural theoreticians. I wrote it at home, in libraries, in cafés and on trains. I even wrote it on a family holiday in Italy, typing on a wobbly table crusted with dried tomato sauce in a lakeside hotel. All the anecdotes and stories that I rejoiced to include in this book – tales of the Mafia threatening to drive a falconer out of New York City because his falcon was a threat to their pigeon-flying activities, stories of fan dancers, jet pilots, astronauts and the diplomatic shenanigans of early modern royalty – these were things that didn't fit in my PhD. But they fitted here. And weaving facts and anecdotes and images together to discuss aspects of our place in the world through the lens of our relationship with falcons – that was a fascinating and deeply absorbing task.

I chose to write about falcons rather than hawks because, as I say in *H is for Hawk*, they were the birds I most loved and was most familiar with; placid, devastatingly beautiful aerial predators. They're not much like goshawks, though much of their cultural history is shared with these powerful and highly strung accipiters. But oddly enough, it was an encounter with a goshawk after this book came out that, in retrospect, was part of the complicated mesh of happenstance that brought me to Mabel, my own goshawk.

It was in the autumn of 2006, in Uzbekistan, a few short months before my father died. I'd driven with a group of other fieldworkers in a Russian jeep down to the banks of the Syrdarya river in Andijan province, where water described a lazy loop through poplar forest and feathery grey tamarisk. Once we'd pitched our tents, I went for a stroll in the hot, blank forest sunlight. It was very still and quiet; just the constant pattering of dry, falling leaves. My feet crunched on salt-crusted mud and across leaf litter sparking with grasshoppers and sinuous silver lizards. After a mile or so, I found myself in an open clearing and looked up. And that is when I thought I saw a man standing in a tree. That's what my brain told me, momentarily. A man in a long overcoat leaning slightly to one side. And then I saw it wasn't a man, but a goshawk. Moments like this are very illuminating. I'd never thought before, much, about the actual phenomenology of human–hawk resemblance, which must have brought forth all those mythological hawk–human bonds I've studied for so long, the ones I'd written about in this book. Everything I'd written about this strange symbolic connection between hawks and human souls felt as if it had a different kind of truth, now, one forged of things other than books. I looked up at a hawk in a tree, but I saw a man. How curious. This goshawk must have been 80 feet away, so dark against the bright sun I couldn't see whether he was facing me or the river. His short head and snaky neck craned: he was looking at me. I raised my binoculars to my eyes as slowly as I could, half-closing my eyes so my lashes fringed the glare. There. There he was. The glare wasn't so bad. I could see his edges very clearly. The light was very bright. But I could also faintly see the horizontal barring on his chest feathers. This was an adult male goshawk, and he looked very different from the ones at home. He had a dark, dark head with a flaring pale eyebrow, and the bars on his chest were close-set and far from the thick, broken lines of European birds. Imagine tracing – with a ruler – each horizontal line of a narrow-ruled notebook with a thick, dark-grey felt-tip pen. That's what his front looked like, through the glare. And he was standing on a bare branch and making up his mind what I was, exactly, and what he should do about it. Slowly, he unfolded his wings, as if putting on a coat, and then, rather quietly and leisurely, he took to the air, one long leg and loosely clenched foot trailing as he went. I was astonished by how long-winged he was, and how much he looked like a big – albeit long-tailed – falcon. His shape was very different from the goshawks at home. This was a migrant hawk, one who had travelled down mountains and across plains to find himself here and at home.

It wasn't until that dark year with my own hawk Mabel that the visceral truth that we use nature as a mirror of our own needs became something I *understood*, rather than merely *knew*. But even so, that sighting of a goshawk in Uzbekistan was the start of my education, the start of understanding the difference between knowing something intellectually and feeling it deep in your bones. That migrant goshawk, and that momentary lapse of focus that made me see him as a person, not a bird – I wonder, now, if he was also part of the reason I cleaved to a goshawk after my father's death. And I wonder if there would have been any Mabel at all had I not thought so long and so hard about the meanings of raptors as I wrote this book.

The falcons that fly in these pages shine a light upon human culture as much as they do upon their own biology and behaviour. I am passionately of the opinion that it is crucial for us to try to understand what lies behind the meanings we have given, and continue to give, to wild animals, including hawks and falcons. It's a project that teaches us about human minds and cultures and the complicated workings of social history, natural history, art and science. But most of all, and now more than ever before, it is essential that we look long and hard at how we view and interact with the natural world for other reasons. We are living through the world's sixth great extinction, one caused entirely by us, through habitat loss, climate change, chemical contamination of ecosystems by pesticides and herbicides, and urban and agricultural development. Piecing together how and why we see landscapes and creatures as we do, how we value them and why we think we should protect them – these are questions whose importance is far and above mere academic interest. They are questions to which the answers are simply about how we can save the world.

Opposite: Gouache of a gyrfalcon from a mid-15th-century Persian album of paintings and calligraphy.

'Ringed with the azure world': peregrine falcon and skydiver.

Introduction

IN 1998 KEN FRANKLIN TRAINED a young female peregrine falcon called Frightful to follow a free-falling speed-suited skydiver out of an aircraft door at 16,000 feet. In a series of dives, high-speed film footage showed the falcon in her element, tucking her head deep into her collarbones, feet sleek beneath her feathers, moulding herself into the perfectly aerodynamic profile of a raindrop. At speeds of over 100 miles an hour, the minutest alterations to her body shape or wing profile gave punishingly exaggerated effects; she looked, as Franklin later described, shrink-wrapped, mummified. And just as it seemed impossible for her to fall any faster, she'd change her shape again. Shrugging one shoulder sharply forward to slice through the molecules of resistant air, she dropped away from the astonished cameraman, cutting the sky in two at a velocity of over 200 miles an hour.

Falcons are the fastest animals that have ever lived. They excite us, seem superior to other birds and exude a dangerous, edgy, natural sublimity. All this means nothing to falcons, of course; these are our own concepts. Though real, living animals, falcons can't be seen except through what anthropologist Franz Boas described as your *Kulturbrille*, the invisible mental lens your own culture gives you through which you see the world. All encounters with falcons are in a strong sense encounters with ourselves

– whether the falcons are real or imaginary, whether seen through binoculars, framed on gallery walls, versified by poets, flown as hunting birds, spotted through Manhattan windows, sewn on flags, stamped on badges, or seen winnowing through the clouds over abandoned arctic radar stations.

Animals are so malleable a repository for human meanings that some modern critics see them as existing almost entirely within the realm of human representation. But falcons are not merely imaginary receptacles for symbolic meaning. They live, breed, fly, hunt, breathe. Pigeons have no illusions that falcons are merely empty signifiers filled with meaning by humans. And as living animals, real falcons constrain, undercut and sometimes resist the meanings people have attached to them.

The broad-shouldered, solid form of a falcon sitting silently on a dead tree or a rocky outcrop has an unmistakable, magnetic gestalt and, when it takes flight, a power and ease in the air that does strange things to the susceptible viewer. In their presence, confessed 1950s nature writer W. Kenneth Richmond, 'we may as well acknowledge the fact that we are inferior beings ... Terror and beauty, cold silver and hot blood are fused in them to produce the natural aristocrat', before adding defensively, 'at least so it has always seemed to me'.[1] Falcon watching might be addictive, but the lure of falcons can become far more than a vocation. Writer Stephen Bodio knew a man who showed his trained falcon to visiting Jehovah's Witnesses. '*This* is what I worship,' he told them proudly.[2] Such unexpected religiosity reaches its highest pitch in *The Peregrine* by J. A. Baker. This classic of natural-history writing is a diary of one man's obsessive quest for wild peregrines across the winter landscapes of East Anglia. An ecological *Confessions of St Augustine* or modern-day Grail-search, these are at heart the diaries of a soul's journey to grace, a man

The white gyrfalcon, for millennia the most revered and sought-after falcon of all. Trapped on the coast of Greenland as part of a study of falcon migration, this female is about to be released by field biologist Erin Gott.

looking for God. The style is episodic and ornate: Baker searches for the peregrine day after day, every sighting imbued with deep personal significance. He finds traces of where the peregrine has been – old kills, a few feathers. He searches for the right clothes, the right rituals and actions to allow him to get ever closer, suffering privations and hardships on his way. He envisions the landscape as animated entirely through the falcon's power, creating life from the still earth by conjuring flocks of birds into the air. He assumes humility – and these become the diaries of a man seeking to become invisible, growing so familiar to the falcons he sees on his daily treks that they trust him as part of the landscape he and they both move upon. And finally, at the end of the book, as night falls, an epiphany. Baker is gripped by a sudden certainty that he would find the peregrine by the coast – an irresistible inward call that sends him out into a bleak near-night on a quest through a desolate landscape. And there he finds the falcon. He slowly approaches until he stands right before it. It is roosting in a thorn bush. It accepts his presence, closes its eyes and returns to sleep. And Baker is fulfilled.

What is this animal that provokes so much emotion? In the first chapter I sketch out some of the biological and ecological dimensions of falcons, and in the rest of the book explore how people have responded in such a curiously strong manner to something that, after all, is just a bird.

one

Natural History

THE 60-ODD SPECIES of the falcon family Falconidae superficially resemble but are probably only distantly related to the other diurnal birds of prey such as hawks, eagles and vultures; some researchers think they are more closely related to owls. They are very variable in shape and habit. From the garbage-can-raiding, raucous, vulture-like caracaras to the secretive tropical forest falcons, all share certain features, such as a bony tubercle in the nostril and a unique moult pattern, which mark them as members of this family. And taxonomically nested within the Falconidae are the 'true falcons' of the genus *Falco*. These species are thought to have evolved relatively recently, perhaps seven or eight million years ago when climatic changes opened up millions of acres of new savannah and steppe grassland. A rapid, explosive radiation of forms occurred to take advantage of these open landscapes.

Falco is often subdivided into four groups: the largely insect-ivorous hobbies, the tiny, bird-killing merlins, the kestrels, and the group with which we are directly concerned, the large falcons, which can be further divided into two groups, the peregrines and the desert falcons. Both are fast-flying, dark-eyed, active hunters of open airspace. The peregrines specialize in avian prey, while the desert falcons also take mammals, reptiles and insects. In common with many bird-catching raptors, both groups show reversed size dimorphism (RSD): that is, females are considerably larger than males. Evolutionary ecologists have been trying to account for this for years. Perhaps females prefer smaller males because they present less of a threat to themselves and their young. Or perhaps aggressive female competition for males who hold the best breeding territories has selected for large females. Another theory sees RSD as allowing the exploitation of a wider range of prey – with males specializing in catching smaller, more agile birds and females in catching larger, less manoeuvrable ones – but this does not explain why females, rather than males, should be the larger of the two. Tiercel, the falconry term for a male falcon, is from the Old French *terçuel*,

A young peregrine in flight, showing the long-pointed wings and dark cheek markings so typical of the genus *Falco*.

Portrait of an adult peregrine falcon. This wild female is looking through an office window in Toronto, Canada.

derived from the Latin *tertius* meaning a third; males are generally about a third smaller than females.

Western science counts around ten species in this large falcon group, but exactly how they are related and whether particular forms should be considered full species, subspecies or mere races of other species is a scientific conundrum. Such confusion is not helped by the discovery that captive-bred hybrids between some species, such as gyrfalcons and saker falcons, are fully fertile. What is the point of worrying about precise definitions of species, one might ask; falcons existed for millions of years before we started fretting about how to classify them. But these taxonomic decisions have real-world implications. Conservation requires stable definitions of the things we are trying to conserve; species or other units must be legally defined. Many falcon populations are

Young peregrine falcons have streaked underparts, as seen in this early 19th-century Indian watercolour in the Tanjore style.

threatened by loss of habitat or by direct persecution, but these population types may 'fall through the net' of Western taxonomy, as in the case of the saker falcon, a species in which the non-coincidence of scientific and folk taxonomies is distinctly problematic. Western science describes two to five subspecies of the saker. Arab falconers, however, use a complex taxonomy based on size, colour and conformation, such as *ashgar* (white), *aukthar* (green), *jerudi* (barred), *hurr shami* (red), and so on. In post-Soviet Russia, illegal smuggling of particularly favoured colour forms for the Arab falcon market exerts disproportionate pressure on populations that cannot be granted greater legal protection than others because they remain outside the scientific categories of Western conservation.

THE PEREGRINES

The peregrine, wrote W. Kenneth Richmond, is a bird of 'perfect proportions and finely cut features, daring and intelligence, spectacular performance in the air and matchless execution in the chase – it has them all, a natural aristocrat'.[1] Here the falcon sounds more like a John Buchan hero or a Second World War flying ace, but the effusive fashioning of this falcon into the discourse of nobility has a long heritage. In Iran and Arabia, the peregrine is called *Shaheen*, Farsi for 'emperor'. Pero López de Ayala, Chancellor of Castile and medieval Spanish authority on falconry, thought it 'the noblest and best of the birds of prey, the lord and prince of hunting birds'.[2] And 700 years later the American ornithologist Dean Amadon rather oddly conflated concepts of adaptive fitness with sheer admiration when he called it the finest of falcons and assumed it must therefore be the most highly evolved of the *Falco* group. The name 'peregrine' comes from the Latin *peregrinus* 'wanderer'; if we assume the mantle of a geopolitician, and measure success by the extent of territory held, *Falco peregrinus* is the most successful bird alive. Except for Antarctica, Iceland and some oceanic islands, the species is found on every continent and in a huge variety of forms. These range in colour from the pallid, white-fronted morph of the Chilean peregrine *F. p. cassini* to the dark Madagascar peregrine *F. p. radama*. Peregrines from humid, tropical latitudes tend to be darker and more richly coloured than those from arid or northerly regions. Desert peregrine types include the tiny blue and rust-coloured broad-shouldered Barbary falcon *F. pelegrinoides* from North Africa, and in the mountains of Iran and Afghanistan, the red-naped shaheen *F. p. babylonicus*. In Iran this bird is called the *Shaheen-e kuhi*, the shaheen of the hills, as opposed to the *Shaheen-e bahri*, the shaheen of the sea, the migratory Arctic peregrine that winters on the Iranian coasts.

THE DESERT FALCONS

The largest falcon, and arguably the most impressive, is a member of a softer-plumaged subgroup of *Falco* known familiarly as the desert falcons, for these species generally inhabit arid regions. The gyrfalcon *Falco rusticolus* is a hulking great bird; females are nearly the size of a small eagle. Gyrs live in the arctic and sub-arctic where prey can be scarce and water is locked into ice for

A grey-phase gyrfalcon tail-feather.

A white gyrfalcon attacking a tundra swan. Scroll painting on silk by Yin Xie, Ming period.

much of the year; they are well adapted for the exigencies of this habitat, with thick, deep plumage and shaggy lower-breast feathers that entirely cover their feet when they sit; they will bathe with relish in freshly thawed snow. They hunt mainly ptarmigan, lemmings and Arctic hares, but they will eat fish and scavenge from frozen carcasses.

Gyrs have a number of colour-phases broadly correlated with their geographic origin. The *obsoletus* birds of boreal North America are almost black. Grey and silver forms are found throughout their range. From northern Greenland and Kamchatka come brilliant white birds with black-barred scapulars and wing feathers, called *candicans*. In seventeenth-century Spain these birds were called *Letrados* because the marks on their backs looked like the marks of a pen. The gyrfalcon's size and beauty have granted it high status in all falconry cultures; in medieval Europe it was particularly favoured for flights at large quarry such as the red kite (*Milvus milvus*) and crane (*Grus grus*).

Today gyrs are occasionally given as gifts to Gulf States dignitaries by governments and oil companies, but from the eleventh century until the eighteenth they were among the most valuable of diplomatic gifts. In 1236 Edward I of England received eight grey and three white gyrfalcons from Norway. He immediately sent four of the grey gyrs to the king of Castile, apologizing that he could not send white falcons, for only recently he had lost

Hermann Goering's white gyrfalcon, in an oil by falconer-artist Renz Waller.

The saker falcon, the traditional species of Arab falconry.

nine of his own. And they were frequently used in diplomatic negotiations. Charles VI of France sent Norwegian gyrfalcons to Bajazet as a ransom for the marshals de Boucicault and de la Tremoille after the battle of Nikopol in 1396, while the Duke of Burgundy brought about the liberation of his son, the Duke of Nevers, by sending his Turkish captors twelve white gyrfalcons. In the 1930s Hermann Goering planned to release white gyrs in the German Alps. He was convinced that this, the largest and most powerful of falcons, must have had its ancestral home in Germany. The ideological underpinnings of this ecological introduction are, to say the least, uncomfortable, and Renz Waller's portrait of Goering's own white gyrfalcon bathed in mountain

A 19th-century
lithograph by
Joseph Wolf of
lanner falcons:
an adult in front,
an immature bird
(eating a quail)
behind.

sunlight is disturbingly true to the artistic conventions of National
Socialist portraiture.

Another desert falcon, the saker falcon *Falco cherrug,* is the
traditional bird of Arab falconry. Trapped in the autumn on
migration across Arabia to wintering grounds in East Africa, the
bird was known to Bedouin falconers simply as *saqur* 'falcon'.
Sakers nest in steppe grassland and in open forests from eastern
Europe across Asia. Like the gyr, they occur in a wide variety of
forms. Plain-backed, brown, Western lowland birds become
larger, more rufous in colour and barred in the Eastern highland

forms. But this clinal distribution is only a broad trend; saker populations include spotted or barred, brown, grey, burnt orange, almost black birds and birds bleached by the sun to near white. The Altai falcon *Falco altaicus* is a dark gyr-like bird from the Russian Altai, known as *Turul* in Mongolia. In India and Pakistan the desert falcons are represented by the laggar falcon *Falco jugger*, a soft-plumaged brown and cream falcon that preys on lizards as well as birds and small mammals. In the arid and semi-arid regions of Africa and southern Europe, its counterpart is the steel-blue and salmon-pink lanner falcon, *Falco biarmicus*. An avian specialist, the lanner often ambushes desert birds at waterholes and is renowned in falconry for its pleasant temperament. The sixteenth-century falconer Edmund Bert boasted that

A New Zealand falcon on South Island. The only falcon species native to New Zealand, it is threatened by habitat destruction and by the nest-raids of introduced possums.

his trained goshawks were as 'sociable and familiar as a lanner'.[3] Conversely, the North American prairie falcon *Falco mexicanus* is a celebrated malcontent in falconry, known for its foul temper. It inhabits the plains and deserts of the American West. Although it bears a superficial resemblance to the saker falcon and is traditionally assigned to the desert falcon group, recent genetic studies have suggested that the species is more closely related to the peregrine.

Australasia is home to a number of large falcons hard to assign to either desert falcon or peregrine category, such as the black falcon *F. subniger* and grey falcon *F. hypoleucos*. Other Australasian falcons have evolved to exploit predatory niches elsewhere filled by hawks and buzzards, the hawk-shaped New Zealand falcon *F. novaseelandiae*, in particular. Along with a few other large falcon species, these appear less often in this book because their cultural history is less rich than the species previously discussed, either because their relationship with indigenous communities is lamentably undocumented or because they have little contact with humans at all. For example, the richly coloured, huge-footed, orange-breasted falcon *F. deiroleucos* is a species whose mysteriousness is, in part, a function of biologists' difficulty in finding it in its remote South American forest habitat.

WHAT IS IT LIKE TO BE A FALCON?

Claiming to understand the life-world of another person is philosophically suspect; for a different animal, the attempt is perhaps absurd – but undeniably fascinating. Our commonsense anthropomorphism suggests that the world the falcon experiences is probably rather like ours, only more acutely perceived. But from the available evidence it seems that the falcon's sensory world is as different from ours as is that of a bat or a bumblebee. Their high-speed sensory and nervous systems give them extremely fast reactions. Their world moves about ten times faster than ours, so events in time that we perceive as a blur, like a dragonfly zipping past our eyes, are much *slower* to them. Our brains cannot see more than 20 events per second – falcons see 70–80; they are unable to recognize the 25-pictures-per-second moving image on a television screen. Seeing things closer together in time than we do allows them to stretch out a foot at full speed to grab a bird or a dragonfly from the air.

When fixing their eyes on an object, falcons characteristically bob their head up and down several times. In so doing they are triangulating the object, using motion parallax to ascertain distance. Their visual acuity is astonishing. A kestrel can resolve a 2-millimetre insect at 18 metres away. How is this possible? Partly through the size of the eyes: these are so huge that the back of each orb presses into the other in the middle of the skull. The retina is avascularized to prevent shadows or light-scattering;

The morphology of the peregrine falcon, by Joseph Wolf. Note the tomial tooth on the beak, used to break the neck of prey.

instead of blood vessels, nutrients are supplied to the retinal cells from a projecting, pleated structure called the pectin. Falcons' visual sensory cells, the rods and cones, are far more densely packed than ours, particularly the colour-sensitive cones. While we have around 30,000 cones in the most sensitive part of the retina, the fovea, raptors have around 1 million. Moreover, each of their photoreceptive cells has individual representation in the brain. Associated with the cone cells are coloured oil droplets that are thought to sharpen contrast and pierce haze, or may protect those cells from ultraviolet radiation. While humans have one fovea, falcons have two – thus, two images of a single object focused on these foveae may fuse in the brain and produce a true stereoscopic image. Furthermore, between these two foveae, there is a horizontal streak of increased sensitivity, a kind of 'smeared fovea' running between them. This allows falcons to scan the horizon without moving their heads. But not only do falcons see more clearly than humans, they also see things *differently*. They are believed to see polarized light, useful for navigating in cloudy skies. They also see ultraviolet. Overall, falcons have a radically different phenomenal world. Humans have three different receptor-sensitivities – red, green and blue; everything we see is built from these three colours. Falcons, like other birds, have *four*. We have three-dimensional colour vision; they have four. It is hard to comprehend. Dr Andy Bennett, researcher in the field of avian vision, considers the difference between human and bird vision as being of the same order as that between black-and-white and colour television. In the barest of functional terms, a falcon is a pair of eyes set in a well-armed, perfectly engineered airframe.

The beak is extremely powerful; anyone who has been bitten by a falcon will vigorously attest to this. A sharp projection on the upper mandible fits neatly into a notch in the bottom mandible.

This 'tomial tooth' is used to sever the vertebrae of prey, an efficient method of administering the *coup de grâce* to avoid a tussle on the ground and broken feathers. Beak dimensions vary between species and sexes. Southern latitude peregrines have proportionately more massive beaks than northern birds. Once thought to be an adaptation for killing dangerous prey such as parrots, the reasons for this gradient are obscure. There is, however, a strong correlation between foot shape and prey type. Bird-killing species such as the peregrine and lanner have relatively short legs to withstand the impact of hitting prey at speed; their toes are long and thin. On the underside of each toe are warty pads of skin that fit closely against the curve of the talon when the foot is clenched, giving the bird secure purchase on feathers. Sakers and gyrs have proportionately thicker, shorter toes and longer legs, a better arrangement for catching mammalian prey in snow, grass or steppe scrub. The toes have a 'ratchet' tendon mechanism: after the initial effort of clenching the foot, falcons can hold them locked shut with no muscular effort, an invaluable strategy for carrying prey in flight or sleeping on a branch in high winds. At rest, falcons habitually tuck one foot up underneath their feathers. There, it is often invisible. Visitors to falconry centres often ask staff why they have so many one-footed falcons.

The skeleton is light, strong and highly adapted for the demands of flight. Some bones are fused. Major bones are hollow, air-filled and reinforced by bone struts. These pneumatized bones are connected to the bird's respiratory system. *Really* connected: a bird suffering a compound fracture of a wing or leg can breathe through the exposed end of the bone. The massive flight muscles, making up around 20 per cent of the weight of a peregrine, are attached to the sternum, or 'keel', and are served by oxygen from a highly efficient respiratory system. Rather than an in–out lung

Peregrine falcon skeleton.

system like ours, air is drawn continuously and in one direction through the lungs via a series of nine thin-walled air sacs throughout the body; these also have a thermo-regulatory function. Overall, falcons' respiratory and circulatory systems are far more efficient than ours; despite the far greater metabolic rate of falcons, they breathe at about the same rate we do.

Compared with other birds, a falcon's digestive system is short, for flesh is easily digested. Falcons cannot digest feathers and fur; these are stored in the crop and ejected from the mouth in the form of a tightly packed 'casting' some hours later. They drink infrequently, for most of the moisture they require is derived from their prey and their water economy is impressive; falcon faeces – 'mutes' or 'hawk chalk' in falconers' parlance – are composed of faecal matter and a chalky suspension of uric acid crystals. Falcons can excrete uric acid 3,000 times more concentrated than their blood levels. That's acidic enough to etch steel.

FLIGHT

What of flight, the single most celebrated falcon characteristic? Falcon bodies are heavy in relation to their wing area. Their flight profile is unstable and anhedral – that is, '∧'-shaped, the opposite of the 'v'-shaped dihedral attitude of soaring vultures and eagles. Their wings have a high aspect ratio – the ratio between wingspan and wing width – and their low-camber wings are long and pointed. The result is a low-drag conformation more suited to active, flapping flight and fast gliding than soaring. But falcons gain height by powering up on beating wings, or by soaring in rising thermals or updrafts from cliffs or hills. From high perches or from altitudes that may be so high they are invisible from the ground, falcons stoop, or dive, upon prey. Falcon hunting tactics are to be found codified in fighter pilot tactical manuals of the First and Second World Wars – there are only a few places to hide in the sky. Falcons often attack from above by diving out of the sun; Royal Air Force fighter squadrons would assume positions above enemy aircraft formations in order to do the same. Falcons often use the blind spot of their target to approach unnoticed from behind and beneath and fly their target down. Similarly, RAF 'fighter area tactics' in the Battle of France called for fighter sections to fly into the blind spot of lone bombers, 2,400 feet behind, 100–200 feet below, before attacking. To approach ground prey falcons glide fast, wings motionless, to present a minimal head-on profile. Sometimes they deceive, imitating the flight style of harmless birds in order to approach unsuspecting prey. Once overtaken, prey is either grabbed in mid-air or hit hard with one or both feet. At the speeds attained by stooping falcons, this clout often kills the prey outright.

Falcons living in more enclosed habitats have lower aspect-ratio wings and longer tails, a flight conformation suited for rapid turns in a world of obstacles. This is particularly apparent in the New Zealand falcon, which exploits an ecological niche filled elsewhere by hawks. This aberrant falcon follows prey into trees and even stalks prey on foot through undergrowth. Immature falcons also have longer tails and broader wings than adults, a conformation suited to hunting methods amenable to inexperienced birds: young sakers, for example, will 'quarter' or hover over rodent-rich grassland. After their first moult, their

Long-distance migrant falcons tend to have narrower, longer wings than those of sedentary populations. Here a dark-phase saker flies through a mountain pass in northern Pakistan.

Wing silhouettes of four falcon species. Narrower, longer wings are more suited to aerial attack; broader, rounder wings also allow slow searching flight.

Gyrfalcon

Saker falcon

Peregrine falcon

New Zealand falcon

tails shorten and their wings grow narrower, their feathers stiffer and stronger.

Falcon flight is fast and structurally stressful. Straight-line low-level fast flight in gyrfalcons has been put at 80 mph, but diving peregrines reach well over twice this speed. The bony tubercle in falcon nostrils is often presumed to aid breathing at these high speeds, but it may indicate airspeed by sensing temperature or pressure changes produced by different external air-stream veloci-ties. An extra pair of bones at the base of the tail gives increased surface area for attaching the powerful depressor muscles of the tail – essential for turning and braking sharply in pursuit flights. Such turns exert phenomenal stresses on the bird. The biometrician

Vance Tucker attached a miniature accelerometer to trained falcons to record the G-forces experienced when pulling up near vertically from the bottom of steep dives. As blood drains from their eyes and brains, human pilots may experience total loss of consciousness – G-LOC – pulling around 6 Gs. Eyewitness reports of Tucker's experiments enthuse about how his accelerometer went 'off scale' as the falcons pulled over 25 Gs. At this G-loading, a 2 lb falcon weighs over 60 lb.

Vultures and other slow-soaring fliers have rough, loose body feathers and highly emarginated, splayed primary wing feathers that function as miniature aerofoils to permit low airspeeds. Falcon feathers, however, are tightly contoured; they mould the bird into a sleek shape offering little air resistance. Moulted and replaced once a year, they are of several types: long, stiff attenuated *flight* feathers; insulating *down* feathers; *contour* feathers that cover and smooth the body; bristly *crines* around the beak and cere that shed dried blood after a meal; and barely visible long, hairlike *filoplumes*. These are associated with the flight feathers, and are well served at their bases by nerve endings. Their sensory input is thought to monitor the flow of air over the wing surfaces to allow precise adjustments of wing shape in flight.

Much of a falcon's time is taken up with feather-maintenance; they preen for long periods and bathe frequently. Gently nibbling the uropygial gland just above the tail, preening falcons pick up a fluid of fatty acids, fat and wax and spread it onto their feathers; in addition to waterproofing them, the fluid contains a vitamin precursor that sunlight converts to vitamin D; this is picked up and ingested in the next preening session. As to plumage colour, black, brown, grey, orange and white are typical falcon tones. Lanners, some saker races and most of the peregrine group have bluish upper parts. This blue colouration is common in bird-killing raptors of other species, but no one knows why this should be the case. A characteristic falcon marking is the dark malar stripe that runs down from beneath the eye. In some species it is so extensive that the falcon appears hooded; in a very few, it may be faint or even absent. The stripe appears to combat glare, functionally akin to the dark make-up American footballers wear beneath their eyes. And the bare skin around their eyes and on their legs and cere varies from pale blue or grey to bright orange. These bright colours may be involved in display and mate choice, for immature falcons are far less brightly coloured on their bare parts. First-year falcons also have streaked rather than barred undersides and are browner or paler than adults. The barred and contrast-rich plumage of adults may be associated with territorial signalling, while dull-coloured juvenile plumage allows young birds to wander relatively unpressed through adult territories in the post-fledging and dispersal period.

MIGRATION

Falcon movements can be epic. Acres of text have been written on the whys and wherefores of bird migration. Recent studies indicate that a strong genetic component is involved in the development of migratory behaviour in birds, but an external reason is often straightforwardly apparent for falcon migrations: food. In Kyrgyzstan, sakers move down from the Tien Shan mountains with the first snowfalls in late summer, following their prey to the plains below. Rocky Mountain prairie falcons move to higher altitudes in summer because their main prey at lower levels, Townsend's ground squirrel, hides underground to escape the baking heat. Nomadic movements in response to unpredictable food resources are also found in falcons living in arid zones, such as lanners. Falcons breeding in the arctic migrate thousands of miles each spring and autumn, 'leapfrogging' over resident or partial-migrant birds from mid-latitude populations who live in areas with year-round food. Greenland-nesting peregrines winter as far south as Peru; Siberian peregrines move down to Afghanistan, Pakistan, and as far as South Africa.

Conversely, falcons living in regions where prey is available year-round tend to be sedentary. City peregrines in Manhattan have a year-round source of pigeon food. Peregrines in Britain may use man-made food sources in areas where wild prey is scarce in winter; populations on northern moors have taken advantage of the traditional flight-lines of racing pigeons, much to the dismay of the pigeon-racing community. Peregrines on the humid Queen Charlotte Islands in British Columbia subsist on seabirds; black shaheens in bird-rich tropical Sri Lanka remain at their breeding territories all year.

Migrating falcons move fast, sometimes hundreds of miles a day across land or ocean. One of the copies of *De arte venandi cum avibus*, Frederick II's thirteenth-century *magnum opus*, has an illustration of a peregrine sitting on the rigging of a ship, and gyrfalcons and peregrines still land on ships during migration. On a transatlantic crossing in the 1930s the American biologist-falconer Captain Luff Meredith could hardly believe his luck when he was suddenly presented with a beautiful white gyrfalcon: landing on deck mid-crossing, it had been promptly captured by the crew. Meredith's celebrity falconry status prompted the famous fan dancer Sally Rand to visit him and demand a falcon for her act. Apparently her request was declined.

Clearly, ships are not optimal falcon habitats. But the genus *Falco* is not tied to particular landscapes; that characteristic falcon silhouette can be seen over city centres, deserts and arctic ice-cliffs

A falcon resting on a ship, from Frederick II of Hohenstaufen's 13th-century *De arte venandi cum avibus*. Migrating falcons still perch on ships.

and in the humid air above tropical forests. The large falcons tend to be solitary animals outside the breeding season, although pairs of some species such as lanners hunt cooperatively all year. Lanner falcons in arid regions also congregate in groups at waterholes where prey is concentrated, or may assemble in loose flocks to feed on termite swarms.

Falcons time their breeding to coincide with maximum prey abundance; young falcons are reared and fledge when there is plenty of inexperienced juvenile prey to catch. Most temperate-zone and high-latitude falcons return from their winter territories to their breeding territories early in the year, pair up and lay their eggs in spring. Their breeding territory is generally much larger than the winter territory of single birds, for far more prey is required to feed a family. Its size varies in relation to the availability of prey in the surrounding environment; the breeding territory of the prairie falcon, for example, may be as few as 30 or as many as 400 square kilometres.

This territory may contain several alternate nest sites used from year to year; bare 'scrapes' on ledges, in cliff potholes or on

A peregrine falcon drives a raven from its nesting territory in this engraving by the renowned bird and sporting artist George Lodge (1860–1954).

river cutbanks; or the reused nests of other large birds, such as ravens and eagles. Falcons do not build their own nests. Some peregrine populations nest in trees; one now-extinct population relied on the hollow tops of dead old-growth forest trees in Tennessee. Traditional nest sites can be ancient: gyr eyries in Greenland may go back thousands of years. The Karok people of north-west California considered the peregrine, which they called *Aikneich* or *Aikiren*, to be immortal, for a pair had nested at the summit of *A'u'ich* (Sugarloaf Mountain) since time immemorial. Some British peregrine eyries have been recorded as occupied since the twelfth century, and some, like those of Lundy Island, produced young celebrated for their prowess as falconry birds. There may be some truth underlying such tales of 'special' eyries. Young falcons tend to return to the area where they were reared. This high degree of philopatry may contribute to speciation in the genus, with local genetic traits reinforced over many years.

High nesting densities of otherwise territorial raptors can occur when prey is abundant but nesting sites unevenly concentrated. On the gorges of the Snake River in Idaho, for example, some kilometres from the gorge made famous by Evel Knievel's failed attempt to jump it on a jet cycle, approximately one pair of prairie falcons nests per 0.65 km. These pairs hunt the numerous ground squirrels in the sagebrush desert that extends out from the river gorge. In steppe and prairie grasslands a lack of nest sites may limit falcon populations, even though prey populations may be high enough to support numerous pairs. Conservation management techniques involving the erection of artificial nesting platforms have proved successful in some cases, but some falcons require no such habitat augmentation. Saker falcon ground nests have been found in Mongolia, and there are large

Falcons don't build nests; some species lay their eggs on ledges, while others often use old buzzard or raven nests, like this saker in Mongolia.

populations of ground nesting peregrines in the Arctic. Ground nesting is a dangerous game, exposing eggs and young to predators, and mutualistic relationships with other species have developed. On the Taymyr Peninsula in Siberia otherwise vulnerable ground-nesting peregrine eyries are found in statistically significant proximity to red-breasted goose *Branta ruficollis* colonies. If the vigilant geese spot arctic foxes, or avian predators, their alarm call alerts the falcons, whose aggressive dives to drive away the threat benefit both peregrines and geese.

Large falcons generally breed in their second year or later, but there are numbers of non-breeding adults in the population at any one time. Gyrfalcons may not breed at all in years when lemmings or ptarmigan are scarce. Falcons are generally monogamous; extra-pair copulations are infrequent. Falcon courtship is not marked by colourful plumage; instead, males may perform

dizzying courtship flights near possible nest sites, sometimes
joined by the female. Pair bonding is cemented by males bringing
prey to the female and by elegant nest-ledge displays of bowing
and calling. Frequent copulations – around two or three an hour
before egg laying – further strengthen the pair bond. The single
clutch consists of three to five blotched, rusty brown eggs, which
are incubated by the female for around a month. The young, or
'eyasses', hatch with a thin covering of grey or whitish down that
is replaced by a thicker coat a week or so later. Feather growth is
rapid, quills breaking through the down as young falcons exercise
their wings and their hunting instincts. They are playful in the
nest, grabbing sticks, stones and feathers in their feet, turning
their heads upside down to watch buzzing flies and distant birds,
pulling on the wings and tails of their irritated siblings. They take
their first unsteady flights aged around 40 to 50 days, after which
the parents teach them the rudiments of aerial hunting strategies

Fledgling, or eyass, peregrines, in a well-observed 1895 gouache by the
Finnish artist Eero Nicolai Jarnefelt. The leftmost bird is 'mantling'
protectively over food; the other is calling with the typical hunched
posture of a food-begging youngster.

by dropping dead or disabled prey from a height for the pursuing young to catch.

Young falcons begin killing their own prey and disperse from the territory after four to six weeks, after which their mortality is relatively high. Around 60 per cent of young falcons die in their first year, mainly from starvation. This fact is surprising to many commentators who see falcons as the most efficient predators alive. Surprises like this occur when biology doesn't match mythology – that is, when real animals don't match the ways humans perceive them. Bedouin falconers, for example, who only saw migrating falcons in the desert, never breeding pairs, quite reasonably mapped their own gender concepts onto the falcons they trapped: they assumed that the larger, more powerful birds were male and the smaller, female. But scientific understandings of falcons, too, can be strongly inflected or invisibly shaped by our own social preoccupations. And conservation is riven by conflicts arising because animals possess different values for different cultures. Are falcons paradigms of wildness and freedom? Vermin? Sacred objects? A commercially valuable wildlife resource? Or untouchable and charismatic icons of threatened nature? Investigating these different meanings has real-world implications. People conserve animals because they value them, and these valuations are tied to their own social and cultural worlds. The pictures and stories through which falcons are used to articulate and reinforce different cultural understandings of the world are *myths*, and they are the subject of the next chapter.

two

Mythical Falcons

Detective Tom Polhaus (picks up falcon statue): *Heavy. What is it?*
Sam Spade: *The, uh, stuff that dreams are made of.*
Polhaus: *Huh?*
(closing lines of *The Maltese Falcon*, 1941)

O N A FOGGY NOVEMBER dawn in 1941, the American bird-preservationist Rosalie Edge was woken by the frantic alarm-calls of city birds. She peered from her Manhattan window into Central Park. What had caused this commotion? Blinking back sleep, she realized that the stone falcon she could see carved from a rocky outcrop was no statue. It was alive. Suddenly, time stood still. She was transfixed. My soul, she wrote, 'drank in the sight' of this impossibly exotic visitor to the modern world. Was it, she breathed, the ghost of Hathor, wandered from the Metropolitan Museum and over-taken by sunrise? But no: 'time resumed as the swift-winged falcon swept into the air . . . the enchantment was broken'.[1]

Another ancient falcon worked its enchantments on Humphrey Bogart, Peter Lorre, Sydney Greenstreet and audiences across America that year. The small black statuette of *The Maltese Falcon* casts its dark shadow across the screen at the very beginning of John Huston's *film noir*, and the audience reads the barest bones of its history in scrolling text:

In 1539, the Knights Templar of Malta paid tribute to Charles V of Spain by sending him a Golden Falcon encrusted from beak to claw with rarest jewels ... but pirates seized the galley carrying this priceless token and the fate of the Maltese Falcon remains a mystery to this day.

While driving the plot, the Maltese Falcon remains a mystery. Although it reveals the characters of the people in the film – all of whom desire or fear it – and the worlds in which they live, it is a mute object that reveals nothing more about itself. Likewise, that Central Park encounter at dawn tells us almost nothing about peregrines. But it tells us much about the writer herself and about the era she lived in, revealing some intriguing contemporary attitudes towards nature and history. In wartime America, it seems, falcons could be viewed as mystical manifestations of an age of theriomorphic gods and ancient ritual. But falcons carried

Bogey and the black bird: Humphrey Bogart, the Maltese Falcon and their conjoined shadow in a publicity shot for John Huston's 1941 film.

The falcon as a token of a medieval Golden Age: a detail from a 14th-century fresco by Simone Martini at the church of San Francesco, Assisi.

many other meanings, too. Falcon-enthusiasts such as Edge saw them as living fragments of primeval wilderness imperilled by the relentless encroachment of modernity. Writing about falcons in this period is commonly shot through with a gloomy romanticism akin to that displayed in the works of many contemporary anthropologists who saw the cultures they studied as exotic, primitive, vital and ultimately doomed by historical progress.

And falcons could be icons of history, as well as wild nature. Way back in 1893 a popular magazine described the ancient sport of falconry as having an 'astonishing hold on the popular imagination of Americans' with the image of a hooded falcon 'as firmly impressed on the popular mind as that of St George and the Dragon'.[2] And the Second World War heightened this ability of falcons to conjure a lost golden age of medieval splendour. As America increasingly saw itself as the guardian of a European high-cultural heritage threatened by the dark forces of fascism, trained falcons made frequent appearances in Hollywood epics about the Second World War set in the Technicolor Middle Ages. And wartime falcons could also be seen as the biological counterparts of warplanes: heavily armed natural exemplars of aerodynamic perfection. This notion of falcons fascinated the military. It even led to real falcons being incorporated in defence systems – with varying success, as Chapter Four shows. And, making all too apparent the fact that falcon myths can carry real-world consequences, many Americans, viewing nature with crystalline conviction through their cultural lenses, inserted falcons into their own systems of morality: they viewed them as rapacious murderers of songbirds, enemies to be shot on sight.

All these stories are the falcon-myths of 1940s east coast America. Calling them myths only seems odd because most are still being told. Today, falcons remain precious icons of wild nature; they remain elegant icons of medievalism; some still damn them for their 'cruelty' to other birds, and American F-16 Fighting Falcon jets are familiar silhouettes in many skies. As the saying goes, myths are never recognized for what they are except when they belong to others.

THE FALCON AND THE COCK

Myths, then, are stories promoting the interests and values of the storytellers, making natural, true and self-evident things that are merely accidents of history and culture. They anchor human concepts in the bedrock of nature, assuring their audiences that their own concepts are as natural as rocks and stones. The process is termed *naturalization*, nature being taken as the ultimate proof of how things are. Or how things *should be*: myths have a normative element, too. Sometimes this is obvious: the Kyrgyz proverb 'feed a crow whatever you like, it will never become a falcon', for example, makes inequalities between people natural facts, not merely accidents of society. Fables work similarly to naturalize the storyteller's social mores. But the normative strength of fables is sneakily increased by the way readers are complicit in the myth-making, taking pleasure in working out the moral before reading it themselves. Thomas Blage's 1519 animal fable *Of the Falcon and the Cock* begins with a knight's falcon refusing to return to his fist.

> A Cock seeing this, exalted him selfe, sayeing: What doe I poore wretch alwayes living in durte and myre, am I not as fayre and as great as the Falcon? Sure I will light on hys glove and be fedde with my Lords meate. When he had lighted on hys fiste, the knight (though he were sory) yet somwhat rejoyced & tooke the Cock, whom he killed, but hys fleshe he shewed to the Falcon, to bring him againe to his hand, which the Falcon seeing, came hastily too it.[3]

Blage's moral hammers home the message: 'Let every man walke in his vocation, and let no man exalte him selfe above his degree.' His fable rests on a robust and ancient perception of falcons as noble animals. Refinement, strength, independence, superiority, the power of life and death over others – for millennia these have been assumed features of falcon and nobleman alike. Consequently, falcon myths often reinforce human social hierarchies through appealing to the straightforward 'fact' that falcons are nobler than other birds.

In early modern Europe the worlds of humans and birds were thought to be organized in the same way, shaped according to the same clear social hierarchy. Royalty sat at the top of one, raptors at the top of the other, and the class distinctions between various grades of nobility were paralleled by species distinctions between various types of hawks. Often misread by modern falconers as a prescriptive list of who-could-fly-which-hawk, the fifteenth-century *The Boke of St Albans* illustrates this correspondence with sly facility; a kind of *Burke's Peerage* meets *British Birds*:

> Ther is a Gerfawken. A Tercell of gerfauken. And theys belong to a Kyng.
> Ther is a Fawken gentill, and a Tercell gentill, and theys be for a prynce.
> There is a Fawken of the rock. And that is for a duke.
> Ther is a Fawken peregrine. And that is for an Erle.
> Also ther is a Bastarde and that hawk is for a Baron.
> Ther is a Sacre and a Sacret. And Theis be for a Knyght.
> Ther is a Lanare and a Lanrett. And theys belong to a Squyer.
> Ther is a Merlyon. And that hawke is for a lady.[4]

While the existence of this natural hierarchy was unquestionable, those who had sufficient social authority were able to be iconoclastic within its bounds. Thus the Chancellor of Castile, Pero López de Ayala, could declare his preference for the nobly conformed peregrine over the gyrfalcon, for the latter was 'a villein in having coarse hands [wings] and short fingers [primaries]'.[5]

'Ther is a Gerfawken . . . and theys belong to a Kyng'. On his throne, King Stephen feeds a white gyrfalcon. From the *Chronicle of England* by Peter de Langtoft, *c.* 1307–27.

Such notions of parity between hawk and human exemplify that ferociously strong aspect of *Kulturbrille* in which humans assume that the natural world is structured exactly like their own society. A Californian Chumash myth held that before humans, animals inhabited the world. Their society was organized in ways just like that of the Chumash themselves, with Golden Eagle chief of all the animals, and Falcon, *kwich,* his nephew. Such parallels seem obvious. But they may be hidden deep. Sometimes their very existence is surprising – particularly when they occur in 'objective' science. But they are there. Furthermore, ecologists have routinely inflected their understandings of predation ecology with concerns relating to the exercise of power in their own society. Sometimes mappings from human to natural world have assumed moral, as well as functional, equivalences between raptors and humans, particularly in the ways each are respectively supposed to maintain stability in nature and society. This kind of analogical thinking can reach alarming heights. In 1959 soldier, spy and naturalist Colonel Richard Meinertzhagen wrote that the role of birds of prey was to weed out the weak and unfit. Without birds of prey, he maintained, one finds 'decadence reducing birds to flightless condition and often to eventual extinction'.[6] Peace leads to the decline of civilization, for Meinertzhagen. Fear is necessary to maintain social order. Without predators birds 'would become as gross, as stupid, as garrulous, as overcrowded and as unhappy as the human race is today'. 'Where absolute security reigns, as in the pigeons of Trafalgar Square,' he wrote, 'then there is no apprehension. I should dearly love to unleash six female goshawk in Trafalgar Square and witness the reaction of that mob of tuberculous pigeon.'[7] You don't need to have read Nietzsche to comprehend the subtext here, or when Meinertzhagen describes the mobbing of predators by 'hysterical, abnormal, irresponsible' flocks of birds as 'atrocious bad manners'.[8]

TOTEMS AND TRANSFERENCES

For millennia, people wanting to possess qualities their culture considers intrinsic to falcons – power, wildness, speed, hunting proficiency and so on – have assumed falcon identities to do so. Warriors and hunters of the American Southeast Ceremonial Complex lent themselves the falcon's keen eyesight and hunting ability by painting a stylized red-ochre peregrine 'forked eye' design around their own. Falcon beaks were interred alongside arrows fletched with falcon feathers in European Bronze Age graves, perhaps to lend the arrows the speed, precision and lethality of a falcon's flight. Today, a man wearing a falcon t-shirt, a woman wearing a silver falcon necklace, a child grasping a moulted falcon feather tightly after a zoo visit: all these partake of a similar, if less pragmatic, desire to possess falcon qualities by association. But to become falcon-like, neither talismans nor disguises are required: such symbolic transferences can be granted by being named after a falcon or otherwise taking your personal or social identity from one.

In the early twentieth century anthropologists used the term *totemism* to describe the phenomenon in which particular families, clans or groups identify strongly with something non-human, often an animal. The function of animal totems, they wrote, is to allow one group of people to maintain that they are as different from another, otherwise similar group as one species of animal is different from another. For example, in Central Asia, the nomadic Oghuz carefully differentiated between the species, ages and sexes of various birds of prey and used many as emblems, or *ongon*, of their 24 tribes; the *Turul*, or Altai falcon, was the emblem of the house of Attila and was portrayed on Attila the Hun's shield.

Identifications like these have practical and political ramifications. Kyrgyz and Kazakh falconers could give falcons to

This beautiful, anatomically precise copper falcon effigy of *c.* AD 1–350 was found as part of a deposit of Hopewell Culture objects at the Mound City Group, located near present-day Chilllcothe, Ohio.

members of their own families and clans but not to those of others, for doing so would undermine the power of their own. Capturing an enemy's falcon had immense symbolic import. And presenting your own falcon to an enemy was a clear and unambiguous sign of surrender. The legend of Khan Tokhtamysh's famous falcons captures this perfectly. Tamerlane, his arch enemy, wanted to steal eggs from the Khan's falcons, for if he reared chicks from them himself, he reasoned, he could possess his enemy's power. Tamerlane obtained his eggs by bribing the falcon's guard. And indeed, once the falcons were reared, the Khan's powers were lessened: he lost his next battle to Tamerlane and fled. Such notions underpin the long history of falcons as gifts of diplomacy, political settlement and martial negotiation of a value far greater than their rarity or their usefulness as falconry birds would suggest.

The concept of totems fell from favour in the late twentieth century, and for good reason: anthropologists had routinely used it in ways that reinforced their presumptions that totemic societies were 'primitive' compared to their own. But recently cultural historians who study how industrialized societies articulate notions of personal, national and corporate identity have resurrected the term. Falcons can be the collective representation of your family, your clan, your company, your country, your band, your brand. Some falcons are national emblems – the white gyrfalcon depicted on the nineteenth-century Icelandic flag, for example, or the saker on the flag, stamps and banknotes of the United Arab Emirates. Falcon national identities and sporting identities collided in the nineteenth century in the Austro-Hungarian physical education organization Sokol (Falcon), which became a strongly nationalist organization in the interwar period. And falcon totems are frequent in sport. In the 1960s a schoolteacher won a

The Falcons, the US Air Force Academy's American Football team, display their live mascot in a 1950s photo. Real men, it seems, don't need gauntlets to hold falcons.

competition to name Atlanta's football team: the Atlanta Falcons was her suggestion. Her rationale pushed parallels between birds and football players to ludicrous and delightful heights. 'The Falcon is proud and dignified,' she wrote, 'with great courage and fight. It never drops its prey. It is deadly and has a great sporting tradition.'[9]

The notion of falcon as Ur-football player might stretch the symbolic functionality of falcons a little far. But it's par for the

A flying peregrine on a cloth patch for the band British Sea Power.

course; falcons have been used to naturalize such a vast panoply of concepts that it's almost impossible to see where the bird ends and the image begins. Thus falcon totems often carry much broader associative significances. For example, the falcon evokes a special brand of neo-romantic hard-edged pastoralism for the iconoclastic Cumbrian rock group British Sea Power: crowned with leaves, they perform on a stage bedecked with masses of green foliage, a plastic peregrine falcon looming through smoke from the top of an amp, the atmosphere redolent of *Platoon* meets *The Animals of Farthing Wood*.

Hopeful transferences of falcon characteristics also litter the international marketplace, for falcons seem to offer a litany of favoured qualities the world over. A baffling diversity of goods has been named after falcons. Atari's Falcon computer, for example; Falcon bicycles. Publicity shots for the Japanese *Hayabusa* (peregrine) superbike show a falcon sitting on its sculpted handlebars. There are Dassault Falcon corporate jets and Falcon companies selling everything from fishing gear to accountancy skills. The simplicity of this strategy of corporate symbolic transference

Technology meets the family in 1950s America: a Ford Falcon advertisement.

makes it grist for the cynic's mill. *Miami Herald* humourist Dave Barry, for example, described falcons as 'fierce birds of prey named after the Ford Falcon, which holds the proud title of the Slowest Car Ever Built'.[10]

DIVINE FALCONS

Some mythical falcons exist in a world far from bicycles, aircraft and corporate brand hunger. On a pedestal in the Louvre stands a bronze human figure with a falcon's head. His stance – hollow eyes and ruff of feathers above outstretched arms – has been held in bronze for 3,000 years. This is one manifestation of the ancient Egyptian god Horus. Since the popular craze for ancient Egyptian iconography that swept the West after Howard Carter opened the tomb of Tutankhamen, he has become the most familiar mythical falcon of all. Horus means 'the distant one' or 'the one on high'. In pre-Dynastic Egypt his earliest form was worshipped at cities such as Nekhen, known to the Greeks as Hierakonpolis, or Falcon City. This early Horus was a creator god, the celestial falcon who flew up at the beginning of time. His wings were the sky; his left eye was the sun, his right the moon; and the spots on his breast were the stars. When he beat his wings, winds blew.

Ancient Egypt had many falcon gods – war-god Montu, for example, Sokar, Sopdu, Nemty, Dunanwi. As alliances were forged between different regions and cults, many local falcon gods became assimilated to Horus, and Horus to many others. In Heliopolis, the centre of the sun cult, the sky-god Horus merged with the sun-god Re to become the god Re-Hor-Akhty, depicted as a falcon or a falcon-headed man with the sun disk on his head. Horus was also incorporated into Heliopolian cosmogony as the

Horus, the most famous falcon god of all. This bronze, dating from 800–700 BC, was originally part of a scene in which the two Egyptian gods of royalty, Horus and Thoth, faced each other and purified the king with water during ceremonies.

son of the gods Osiris and Isis. In this form he was crowned as the first king of Upper and Lower Egypt. All his human royal successors were known as 'The Horus' during their reign. Real falcons were considered living manifestations of the powers represented by falcon gods, and were deeply involved in Egyptian religious practice. Every autumn a live falcon was ceremonially crowned as the new king at the temple of Edfu, the centre of the Horus cult in Upper Egypt. The statue of Horus presented his new, living heir to the people, and then the falcon was crowned and invested with royal regalia in the temple. This now-sacred falcon was then kept in the nearby grove of the sacred falcons. On its natural death it was mummified and buried with great ceremony.

Hundreds of thousands of falcons in ancient Egypt were mummified and given as votive offerings to the gods. Dipped into tar, or preserved with natron, their bodies were placed in a suitable receptacle or coffin before being passed to the shrine priest to be entombed on the devotee's behalf in mass interment ceremonies. The temple of Nectanebo II at Saqqara, dedicated to Isis, the mother of Horus, contained 100,000 mummified votive falcons stored in galleries, stacked in rows of jars separated by layers of sand. Temple priests bred some sacred animals such as cats and ibises specifically for the purpose of interment, but falcons are difficult to breed in captivity; the Horus cult must have had significant impact on wild falcon populations in the region. The trade in falcons was extensive, and while most of these offerings were indeed local falcon species such as kestrels and lanners, many weren't: kites, vultures and even small songbirds were also interred. Perhaps these were fakes, fraudulently

The father of psychoanalysis, Sigmund Freud, owned this painted figure of a mummified falcon. It represents the Egyptian funerary deity Sokar.

sold to devotees in an ancient deception revealed – along with the birds' frail bones – centuries later by x-ray and magnetic resonance imaging.

FALCON CULTS

Striking parallels exist between the mythico-religious roles of falcons across diverse cultures and over many millennia. As the cult of Horus suggests, falcon-gods are commonly creator-gods and associated with sun or fire. Like Horus, the ancient Iranian fire- and water-god Avestan Xvaranah was depicted as a falcon. Like Horus he was synonymous with the celestial fortune of kings and their divine right to wield authority. God, according to the prophet Zoroaster, had the head of a falcon. The sixteenth-century French falconer Charles D'Arcussia reminded his readers that the ancients thought that the thighbones of peregrines or sakers attracted gold just as a magnet attracts iron. An apt corres-pondence, D'Arcussia thought, because 'the Alchemists . . . attribute golden metal to the sun'. But as a falconer D'Arcussia had a more prosaic explanation. 'The Ancients did not mean any-thing more than that flying hawks is a great expense,' he wrote, 'attracting and consuming much gold from those whose passion for it goes beyond reason.'[11]

Russian anthropologists have traced the existence of these shared falcon myths to a near-universal cult of birds of prey that once existed across ancient Central Asia. They maintain that trade, invasion, migration and settlement carried elements of this cult eastward and westward over millennia. In addition to seeing falcons as creator gods associated with sun and fire, these ancient myths associate falcons with the human soul; they see falcons as messengers between heaven and earth and between humans

Emeshe, the mythological ancestress of the Magyars, is visited by the falcon Turul in a dream.

and gods. They also associate falcons with marriage and fertility. Falcons populate many legends of the foundation of dynasties and empires. Genghis Khan's future mother-in-law dreamt that a white falcon holding the sun and moon in its talons flew down from the sky to her hand. She took the vision as a sign that her daughter would marry the future conqueror. Falcons' association with fertility has its practical uses, too. In parts of Kazakhstan and Kyrgyzstan, trained falcons are traditionally brought inside the yurt during childbirth, for their sharp eyes scare away the demon known as *al-basty* or 'the Red Mother' who attacks women in labour and gives them puerperal fever.

The legends of the giant *Turul* falcon of Hungarian mythology evince many elements common to this cult of raptors. The *Turul* was often depicted as the sun. It was the symbol of the house of Attila, and the ancestor of the Hungarian Árpád dynasty. In 819 King Béla III's royal scribe recorded that the Scythian leader Ügyek married a woman called Emeshe, who bore Álmos, the first of this dynasty of kings:

The boy obtained his name because of the unusual circumstances of his birth, when his mother in a vision saw the great Turul descend from heaven on her and made her fertile. A great spring welled forth from her womb and began flowing westward. It grew and grew until it became a torrent, which swept over the snow-covered mountains into the beautiful lowlands on the other side. There the waters stopped and from the water grew a wondrous tree with golden branches. She imagined famed kings were to be born from her descendants, who shall rule not here in their present lands but over that distant land in her dreams, surrounded with tall mountains.[12]

After this visitation, Emeshe and her son became the first people able to read the will of god from the stars. Like many other elements of this ancient cult, the notion that the first priests were born from the union of a falcon and a woman is firmly located in a shamanic religio-mythical universe. A term borrowed from the

A 7th-century AD Persian silver dish showing a falcon (or perhaps an eagle) carrying a deceased person's soul to the sky. Shown as a naked female figure, the soul feeds the bird with the fruits of her good deeds.

Tungus of Siberia, a shaman is a person who can travel between different worlds during ecstatic trances; in these trances, the shaman's soul leaves his or her body. It can ascend to the upper realms of heaven or down to the underworld; it guides the souls of the dead to heaven, or petitions or negotiates with gods and spirits for knowledge, cures for sickness, predictions of the future and so on.

Falcons often feature as an assisting spirit in shamanic traditions. *Haoma*, 'the drink of immortality', was used in ancient Zoroastrian sacrificial rituals; there's a long tradition of using hallucinogens to achieve these ecstatic trances. Reputedly a preparation of the fly agaric mushroom, *haoma* was stolen from the gods by the falcon and brought to man: falcon images are frequent on ancient Iranian and Persian artefacts and on Achaemenid and Sassanid vessels and weapons. In what is now California, the Chumash people used the *Datura* plant to allow them to contact their personal 'dream helper' spirits. In the early twentieth century, Fernando Librado related how the crew of a Chumash sea canoe were all saved through the intercession of the captain's dream helper, the peregrine, during a storm. Falcons appear as assisting spirits in literature, too: falcons in Serbo-Croatian epic poetry protect their owners by bringing them water in their beaks and shading them from the sun when they are sick.

The world tree is a central element in many shamanic cosmogonies. It bridges heaven, earth and the underworld and often on its topmost branch sits a falcon. The Hungarian *Turul*, for example, perched at the top of the Tree of Life. In Norse legend the falcon was called *Vedfolnir*, 'blown down'. *Vedfolnir* perched on the beak of the eagle that itself sat on the topmost branch of the world tree *Yggdrasil*. This falcon's task was to report to Odin everything he saw in the heavens, on earth and below. Related to

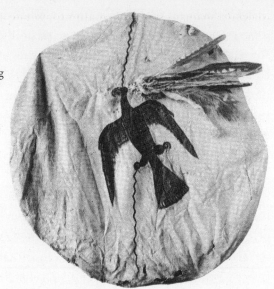

A Crow painted shield cover from Montana with an image of the warrior's protecting genius, the prairie falcon, and an attached bundle of prairie falcon feathers.

the falcon atop the world tree is another frequently encountered shamanic symbol: a bird or falcon perched on a stick. The creation myth of Horus of Edfu describes how the world was formed from chaos when two amorphous beings appeared above a tiny island in the primeval sea. One picked up a stick from the shore, snapped it in two and stuck one half into the ground near the water's edge. A falcon flew out of the darkness and alighted on the stick. Immediately, light broke over chaos, the waters began to recede, and the island grew and grew until it became the earth.

Shamans often transform themselves into birds during their ecstatic trances. In this form they can fly to the world tree to bring back souls as birds, or transport the bird-souls of the recently dead to heaven. The Hungarian *Turul* perched next to the souls of unborn children in the form of birds. As befits shamans with falcon ancestors, shamans can become a falcon on their journeys. Singing chants in honour of the stars, for example,

Malekula shamans spread their arms to imitate a falcon. And in some traditions of the indigenous peoples of the Great Plains of North America, the falcon was the only animal that knew the location of the hole in the sky through which it could reach God. After being asked whispered questions the falcon flew through the hole in the sky and back to deliver the divine replies to the shaman.

SOULS AND UNIONS

Kushlak, the unwise knight, sold his talking falcon to a stranger in exchange for a herd of horses in the Bashkir epic *Kara yurga*. As the stranger took Kushlak's falcon onto his hand, it cried: 'if you give me up, happiness will leave you; prosperity will leave you, your life will leave you. Don't give me away, Kushlak-batir; do not sell me, Kushlak-batir.' Ignoring his falcon's pleas, Kushlak received his herd of horses, and shortly afterwards died. His unlikely death is better understood if we keep in mind the fact that, as D'Arcussia wrote in 1598, 'ancient people used the Falcon to signify the spirit of man'.[13] Right across pre-Christian and pre-Islamic Eurasia, falcons were associated with the human soul. Ancient Turkic gravestones depict the souls of fallen warriors as falcons perching on their hands. The Egyptian *Book of the Dead* describes the deceased as a falcon flying away – and the Egyptian pharoah could adopt the form of a falcon to visit his mortal body after death.

Such associations continue: in some parts of Central Asia killing a falcon is still considered a crime morally equivalent to murder. In the early twentieth century this taboo against harming falcons was still extended to falconers; hurting or humiliating someone carrying a falcon or other bird of prey on the fist was unthinkable. In early twentieth-century California, Three-dollar Bar Billy of the Karuk people maintained that anyone who killed *Aikneich*, the peregrine falcon, would die before the year ended – this had happened recently, he explained, after a man had shot a peregrine, mistaking it for a chicken hawk. 'That year, before leaving', he continued, 'the Aikneich flew around looking at all the towns and houses here and there, and sitting on the houses as if to inspect them.'[14]

The association of falcons with souls and the notion that falcons facilitate communion with heaven or the divine is evoked in numerous mystical traditions. In Sufi mysticism the exiled soul suffers while in mortal flesh and longs to return home to the creator. To become pure enough to rejoin God, one must follow the difficult path of higher and higher levels of spiritual life. Such themes are richly evoked in the work of the great Iranian poet Hafez; in one poem he compares man to a falcon who flies from

A late 17th-century calligraphic prayer in the shape of a falcon by Mohamed Fathiab.

his home to the city of miseries. Christian writers, too, have used falcons in tropes of mystical union. D'Arcussia wrote of how Holy Scripture compares the falcon to the contemplative man who does not embroil himself in worldly affairs and who, 'if at any time there is need for him to descend among them, at once flies back to the sky',[15] and explained that a saintly person is often portrayed through the image of the falcon. In *The Hound and the Hawk,* historian John Cummins elegantly glosses the ways in which St John of the Cross used the theme of the falcon binding to its prey in the skies as a metaphor for his soul's union with God. The falcon's stoop, Cummins writes, 'has two senses: the peregrine's hurtling descent which gives it the momentum to soar up almost vertically, and the individual's self abasement and relinquishing of individuality which enable the soul to rejoin the divine'.[16]

> The nearer I came
> to this lofty quarry,
> the lower and more wretched
> and despairing I seemed.
> I said: 'No-one can reach it';
> and I stooped so low, so low,
> that I soared so high, so high,
> that I grasped my prey.[17]

Mystical unions shade toward erotic unions in falcon tropes, as this medieval Spanish lyric shows:

> To the flight of a heron,
> the peregrine stooped from the sky,
> and, taking her on the wing,

was caught in a bramble bush.
High in the mountains
God, the peregrine came down
to be closed in the womb
of Holy Mary.
The heron screamed so loudly
that Ecce ancilla rose to the sky,
and peregrine stooped to the lure
and was caught in a bramble-bush.

The jesses were long
by which he was caught:
cut from those wobs
which Adam and Eve wove.
But the wild heron
took so slowly a flight
that when God stooped from the sky
He was caught in a bramble-bush.[18]

Lovemaking has frequently been metaphorized as the struggles of falcon and prey. In Turkish songs the love between a virgin bride and her fiancé is couched in terms of the helpless attempts of a female partridge to escape from a falcon. And falconry has irresistibly contributed to erotic falcon myths. Taming falcons and seducing women have long been understood as analogous arts. Many high-school students learn their first falconry from Shakespeare's *The Taming of the Shrew*, where the gentle art of falconry is a trope embedded in the male arts of seduction. As John Cummins delicately phrases it, both activities involve a man's obsessive wish to bend a free-ranging spirit to his own desires, and he quotes a medieval German maxim that 'women and falcons are easily tamed: if you lure them the right way, they come to meet their man.'[19] The metaphor runs both ways: falconry has frequently been couched in erotic terms: novelist David Garnett, for example, described T. H. White's attempts to train a goshawk as reading strangely like an eighteenth-century tale of seduction.

Furthermore, the trappings of falconry – its technologies of control such as hoods, jesses and leashes – working in conjunction with a discourse that often portrays the falcon as mistress and falconer as slave, have allowed it to become figured in explicitly fetishistic and masochistic terms. 'Falconers do it with leather,' proclaimed a 1980s car-sticker. The fabulously baroque and disturbing psychosexual thriller of the same decade, *The Peregrine* by William Bayer, is the *ne plus ultra* of such imaginings. A crazed falconer trains a giant peregrine to kill women; kidnaps a journalist, calls her 'Pambird', decks her in modified falconry equipment crafted by a city sex shop and trains her. 'He

A wry take on gender relations in 1950s America.

took her thus through all the stages of a falcon's training,' says Bayer, 'telling her always that when she was sufficiently trained he would let her fly free and make her kill.'[20] Its final tableau is of a jessed, belled, near-mute and brainwashed woman who has just committed the ritual murder of her captor, standing 'still like a statue, a monolith, an enormous bird, her arms outstretched, her posture hieratic, a cape sewn with a design of feathers falling from her arms like giant wings.'[21]

A happily less explicit story of transformation and desire is found in the Russian folk-tale *Finist the Falcon*. Marya works as housekeeper for her widowed father and two evil older sisters. They ask her father for fineries and silks; she asks for nothing but a feather from Finist the Falcon. Her father finally finds her one; delighted, she locks herself into her room, waves the feather – and a bright falcon hovers in the air before transforming itself into a handsome young man. Her jealous sisters hear his voice and break into her room, but Finist escapes as a falcon through the window. He returns to Marya the next two nights, but alas, on the third night Marya's malicious sisters see him leave, and they fasten sharp knives and needles to the outside of her window frame. The next night the unsuspecting Marya sleeps while Finist gravely injures himself trying to fly into her room. Finally he cries farewell to her with the words 'if you love me, you will find me' and flies away. In the way of such tales, Marya is finally reunited with Finist after a long quest – and of course they live happily ever after.

FALCON TRANSFORMATIONS

A familiar tale of falcon transformation in Indian mythology is the *Sibi-Jâtaka,* in which the gods Indra and Agni test the charity and compassion of the king of the Sibis by changing themselves into a falcon chasing a dove. The terrified, exhausted dove flies into the king's lap and the king offers it protection. But the falcon is outraged. 'I have conquered the dove by my own exertions and I am devoured by hunger!' it exclaims. 'You have no right to intervene in the differences of the birds. If you protect the dove, I shall die of hunger. If you must protect it, then give me an equal weight of your own flesh in return.' The king of the Sibis agrees, commands that scales be brought and places the dove upon them. He cuts some flesh from his thigh with a knife. It is not enough to balance the dove, so he cuts more. Still not enough. The dove grows heavier and heavier as the king cuts flesh from his arms, legs and breast. Finally the king realizes that he must give all of himself, and sits upon the scale. With this, music is heard and a sweet shower of ambrosia falls from the skies to drench and heal the king. Indra and Agni reassume their divine forms, well pleased at his compassion, and announce that the king shall be reincarnated in the body of the next Buddha.

Another divine falcon transformation occurs in Germano-Norse mythology: Freja, goddess of fertility, possessed a falcon-cloak that transformed its wearer into a falcon. But humans, as well as gods, can shape-shift and become falcons. The hero of East Slavic *bylini*, epic warrior-class poems, is a *bogatyr*, a term related to the Turkic and Mongol term *bagadur,* or 'hero'. The *bogatyr* Volkh Vseslavich could change into a bright falcon, a grey wolf, a white bull with golden horns and a tiny ant. Shamanic mythic sources lie deep; the *bogatyr*'s name is related to the Slav term *Volkhv*, signifying 'priest' or 'sorcerer'. In the 1970s Marvel Comics' first black superhero, The Falcon, teamed up with Captain America to fight evil, aided by The Falcon's trained falcon 'Redwing'. Such stories of human–animal transformations have fascinated critics for years: what

The *bogatyr* Volkh Vseslavich assumes the shape of a falcon in a 1927 watercolour by the Russian artist Ivan Bilibin.

do they mean? Do they subvert hegemonic versions of social identity? Question what it means to be human? Articulate religious or gender anxieties? Or are such transformations creating monsters in order to destroy them in fables wrought to reinforce the status quo?

When mere humans assume falcon form, lessons are generally to be learned. The young mage Ged, hero of Ursula K. Le Guin's *A Wizard of Earthsea,* transforms himself into a peregrine, a 'pilgrim falcon' with 'barred, sharp, strong wings', to attack the winged, malevolent demons who have just torn apart his female companion. He flees across the sea, 'falcon-winged, falcon-mad, like an unfailing arrow, like an unforgotten thought'. Ultimately Le Guin's novel is a meditation on the importance of recognizing and accepting one's true self. By manifesting his overwhelming emotions in falcon form Ged puts himself in jeopardy; for the price of shape-shifting is 'the peril of losing one's self, playing away the truth. The longer a man stays in a form not his own,' the text explains, 'the greater the peril.' Pilgrim-falcon Ged seeks out the mage Ogion, his old teacher, and alights on his hand. Ogion recognizes him, weaves a careful spell and transforms the falcon back into human form – a silent, gaunt figure, clothes crusted with sea-salt, with 'no human speech in him now'.

The wizard Ged flies in the form of a falcon: a vignette by Ruth Robbins for Ursula K. Le Guin's 1968 fantasy classic *A Wizard of Earthsea.*

A poster for Wes Anderson's 2001 film *The Royal Tenenbaums*. During filming, the falcon, held here by Luke Wilson, chased a pigeon across New York and was lost for several days.

Ged had taken hawk-shape in fierce distress and rage ... the falcon's anger and wildness were his own, and had become his own, and his will to fly had become the falcon's will ... In all the sunlight and the dark of that great flight he had worn the falcon's wings, and looked through the falcon's eyes, and forgetting his own thoughts he had known at last only what the falcon knows; hunger, the wind, the way he flies.[22]

Those familiar notions of falcons as living concretizations of power, wildness, independence and freedom have afforded them a special role in many fables of self-fulfilment. They operate as figures helping to negotiate the correct balance between civilized human and wild nature. The assistance or aid of a falcon in self-development is elucidated in many modern literary and film representations; here the falcon acts as a balancing alter ego or tutelary animal of a powerless person – often a child stymied by social circumstance or by the emotional absence of a parent. The kestrel in Barry Hines's *Kes*, for example, or the peregrine falcon Frightful in Jean Craighead George's *My Side of the Mountain*, the companion of an urban child who runs away to the Catskill mountains to live wild and recapitulate American history as a modern-day Daniel Boone. Another neglected child, tennis prodigy Richie Tenenbaum in Wes Anderson's 2001 film *The Royal Tenenbaums*, keeps a saker falcon called Mordecai in a mews on the roof of his family home. Set free, Mordecai returns from the New York skies to his fist once an accord is made between father and son. In Victor Canning's novel *The Painted Tent*, sixteen-year-old orphan Smiley, on the run from the police, hides out with a west-country circus family and develops a special bond with a caged peregrine in their menagerie. Fria was a falcon who 'had never known the pure wonder of a peregrine's real flight … the mastery of the air which is the supreme gift of the falcons'.[23] Of all creatures, Smiley 'loved birds because they seemed to carry the real meaning of freedom in their lives' and the peregrine's captivity oppresses him.[24] Fria escapes, and as the book progresses young Smiley's gradual personal empowerment is mirrored by Fria's; she learns hunting skills, revels in the capacity of her freedom; like Smiley she eventually finds a mate.

Another fatherless child unaware of his true identity, the young King Arthur, is transformed into a merlin by his teacher Merlin in T. H. White's *The Sword in the Stone* as part of his 'eddication'. White's portrayal playfully digs at familiar tropes of medievalism; his talking hawks and his Arthurian armoured knights share a social hierarchy, etiquette and iconography. In the mews of the Castle Sauvage, each hawk or falcon is 'a motionless statue of a knight in armour', the birds standing 'gravely in their plumed helmets, spurred and armed'. The parallels are winningly unsubtle and beautifully couched: 'The canvas or sacking screens of their perches moved heavily in a breath of wind, like banners in a chapel, and the rapt nobility of the air kept their knight's vigil in knightly patience.'[25] White gently satirizes the mores of military and sporting elites; before turning the Wart into a merlin and setting him loose into the mews, Merlin suggests that he 'learn by listening to the experts' in the martial culture Arthur will have to live and breathe as king. Merlin points out that these falconry birds:

> don't really understand that they are prisoners, any more than cavalry officers do. They look on themselves as being dedicated to their profession, like an order of knighthood or something like that. You see, the membership of the mews is after all restricted to the raptors, and that does help a lot. They know that none of the lower classes can get in. Their screen perches don't carry blackbirds or such trash as that.[26]

In the 1930s White himself, an unhappy schoolteacher rent by anxieties over his status, his sexuality and his career, quit his job, took a gamekeeper's cottage deep in a wood and set about the task of training a hawk. He saw hawk-training as a form of psychoanalysis, treasuring the notion that he might become a feral creature, like the bird he trained. Indeed, falcons' long, familiar partnership with mankind as falconry birds – often living right inside the most domestic of spheres, the household – coupled with their resistance to domestication, has allowed falcons and other birds of prey to become powerfully charged symbols of wildness in many cultures. Falconry has marked mankind's relation with falcons in myriad robust and decisive ways, and the next chapter explores the phenomenon of what T. H. White called a 'rage that you sleep and drink and tremble to think of . . . even in recollection,'[27] and what King James I described as an 'extreme stirrer up of passions.'[28]

An iconic falconry image: an immature peregrine, wearing jesses,
Lahore bells and a feather-plumed Dutch hood.

three

Trained Falcons

'FALCONRY'S NOT A SPORT, IT'S A VIRUS,' explained the American falconer. Necks craned upward, we watched his trained peregrine climb into a late winter sky. 'A pandemic,' he continued mischievously. 'Appeared in central Asia thousands of years ago and spread all over the place. By medieval times,' he grinned, 'you guys in Europe were in the grip of an epidemic way worse than the Black Death.' His pet theory was succinct, crazy and about par for the course. Falconers routinely pathologize their activity. They say that they never meant to be falconers. That they came under the grip of an impulse they couldn't control. Once a falconer, always a falconer was the maxim of nineteenth-century falconer E. B. Michell. I have heard falconers bemoan how falconry has ruined their careers, destroyed their marriages and occasioned serious heartache, exertion and expense. And do so happily.

Dictionaries define falconry as the use of trained birds of prey to catch wild game. But this singularly fails to capture the social, emotional and historical allure of an activity that has fascinated humans for thousands of years and has taken a most extraordinary variety of forms. Centuries ago, Persian falconers flew peregrines at night, catching ducks flushed from moonlit ponds and marshes; they even trained sakers to catch such unlikely quarry as eagles and gazelles. Louis XIII caught sparrows with

Queen Kristina of Sweden (*r.* 1632–54) and her falconer, in a
mid-17th-century oil painting by Sébastien Bourdon.

trained grey shrikes in the gardens of the Louvre; at dusk he
hawked bats with peregrines. But in scale, form and social nature,
falconry is just as varied a pursuit today. In fragrant desert,
American falconers search out the largest and most spectacular
quarry for trained falcons, the sagegrouse. Arab VIPs land with
their falcons in glossy private jets on dedicated landing strips in
Pakistan. On Scottish moors, tweed-clad and rain-soaked figures
tramp across heather to fly red grouse with their peregrines. In

Zimbabwe, pupils at Falcon College have even trained falcons as part of their school curriculum.

Some see falconry as an anachronistic pursuit, an irrelevant pastime beloved of historical re-enactment fanatics. It's easy to see why; media coverage of falconry tends to linger on its ancient and venerable history. But falconry has a vibrant present. In some countries it's a part of everyday life: falcons are carried in local marketplaces and malls to tame them in the United Arab Emirates. American falconers see themselves as living in a new golden age of falconry. In Britain, falconry is more popular today than at any time over the last three centuries: no country show is without its falconry display, and British radio's oldest soap-opera *The Archers* has its falconer. Falconry centres and schools have opened across Britain and Europe. International, national and local falconry clubs thrive. The inimitable Martha Stewart, doyenne of American interior design, has even appeared on television with a peregrine on her gloved fist. Whether this is a high or a low point in falconry's history is moot. Falconry is very much alive.

WHY AND WHEN?

Humans have used falcons as hunting partners for at least 6,000 years, perhaps more: no one agrees on when, where or how falconry began. Each falconry culture has its own creation myth that invariably locates the birth of falconry in past societies that reflect its own cultural preoccupations. In 1943, for example, Harvard professor Hans Epstein maintained that falconry was a mark of civilization, requiring a 'wealth of leisure, great patience, sensitivity and ingenuity, not ordinarily shown with regard to animals by primitive people'.[1] He was sure, therefore, that it could

Young falcons in the desert near Abu Dhabi. Falcon training here takes place in the morning and evening; when the sun's heat becomes too great, the falcons rest in the shade.

not possibly have a Germanic origin. The Trojans were the first falconers, thought many sixteenth-century Europeans. Nineteenth-century British falconers with good classical educations seized on Pliny's brief description of Thracian bird-catchers using hawks to drive wild birds into nets as proof that falconry began in ancient Greece, even though Xenophon's exhaustive essay on Greek hunting, *Cynegeticus*, mentions falconry not once.

Recent discoveries of raptor bones in Near East Palaeolithic graves lead some to suggest that falconry has a prehistoric origin. But most modern commentators think that it first arose on the high plateaux of Central Asia. From there it was carried east, arriving in China and Japan in the third century AD, and west with trade and invasion all the way to Western Europe. Of course, falconry could have arisen independently in several places. Cortez reported that Montezuma kept large collections of birds of prey at the Aztec court, although whether or not they were used for falconry is hotly debated. Arab scholars have written that the first man to train a hawk to hunt was al-Harith bin Mu'awiyah bin Thawr bin Kindah, back in pre-Islamic times. Marvelling at a falcon accidentally caught in a bird-catcher's net, he took it home and carried it about perched on his arm. One day the falcon left his arm and caught a pigeon, the next day, a hare – and falconry was born. And falconry has the honour of being sanctioned in the Holy Koran:

> They ask you what is lawful to them. Say all good things are lawful to you, as well as that which you have taught the birds and beasts of prey [*Jarih*] to catch, training them as Allah has taught you. Eat of what they catch for you, pronouncing upon it the name of Allah. And have fear of Allah: swift is Allah's reckoning.

In the 1930s British falconer Colonel Gilbert Blaine tried to explain the strange hold falconry had over him and his fellows.

A terracotta figure of a falconer from 6th-century Japan.

He declared that the 'true falconer is born, not made'. 'Deeply rooted in the nature of certain individuals [exists] some quality which inspires a natural liking for hawks,' he continued. Musing on what this quality might be, he concluded that it must be 'an instinct inherited from our ancestors' who pursued the sport.[2] Rather winningly, Blaine then awards himself and his friends a fortunate lineage. For the ancestors of the modern-day 'true falconer' were all aristocrats. 'No uncultured race has ever attempted to explore [falconry's] mysteries', he wrote; 'even among the cultured peoples the use and possession of the noble falcons were confined to the aristocracy, as an exclusive right and privilege.'[3]

THE FALCONS IN FALCONRY

Blaine's words are mired deep in his own social preoccupations, but his notion that falcons are aristocratic birds is a constant across most falconry cultures. 'Their calm behaviour, noble, cool appearance and reliability is what sets the falcons apart from all other hawks,' wrote American falconer Harold Webster in the 1960s, his sentiment well-nigh indistinguishable from that of early modern falconers and loaded with just as normative a social component. 'It always has and always will. There is nothing quite comparable to them.' He described hunting with falcons as a highly social affair, 'spacious, noisy, spectacular, beautiful and exciting'. And consequently 'it has its highest appeal to the extrovert who likes to be out with friends and in company.'[4] As in foxhunting today, hawking with falcons in early modern Europe was a grand social occasion requiring a large entourage and vast tracts of land to be seen at its best. And again, Webster is heir to centuries of social positioning in falconry when he writes that the

Holding a gyrfalcon, and dressed in sable fur and red leather,
this is Robert Cheseman, falconer to Henry VIII, in a painting
by Hans Holbein the Younger, 1533.

man who shuns falcons and prefers hunting with short-winged
hawks such as sparrowhawks and goshawks is 'something of an
introvert' who 'prefers to go alone to secret, tangled places along
creekbanks, hedgerows and field edges'.[5] Indeed, in the thirteenth
century, *austringer,* the term for someone who flew hawks rather
than falcons, was a term of abuse.

What, then, *is* this spacious, noisy, spectacular, beautiful and
exciting activity Webster describes? While the sport – or art, or
vocation, or however one chooses to call it – is *falconry*, the activity of hunting using any bird of prey is *hawking*. And you don't
train a falcon to chase quarry – she does so instinctively (in

Western falconry parlance, all falcons are *she*, just like cars and ships and aircraft). The falconer's task is threefold: to tame the falcon; to shape the manner in which she chases quarry; to train her to return should the flight be unsuccessful. No falcons retrieve their prey; should the falcon catch something, the falconer has to run to her and reward her for her efforts, while gently retrieving the dead pheasant, duck or grouse for the pot. After months of work and preparation, the falconer's duty is above all else, as falconer Jim Weaver succinctly put it, 'to provide an opportunity for his falcon to demonstrate its natural abilities to the fullest extent possible'.[6]

AERIAL BATTLES

Falcons are trained to fly in one of two styles – either a direct pursuit of quarry from the falconer's fist, or by diving down onto quarry from a great height. In pursuit flights, or 'out of the hood' flights, the falconer first spies out the quarry before unhooding and releasing the falcon. Arab falconers fly their birds in this way at *hubara* (houbara bustard) and *kurrowan* (stone curlew). These beautifully camouflaged sand-and-rock-coloured birds are hard to spot with the human eye. So Arab falconers often use a spotter falcon, often a wily old saker, to spy out quarry for other falcons to chase. Scanning the horizon, the saker will bob her head, tighten her feathers and stare intently when she has spotted distant quarry.

In modern Europe, pursuit flights are most often seen between falcon and crow, or falcon and rook. Sometimes the quarry *rings up* or climbs hundreds of feet into the air, attempting to keep above the falcon. In turn, the falcon strives to climb above the quarry, so that she can dive, or stoop, upon it. Very high flights in this manner are termed the *Haut Vol* – the Great Flights. They were the *ne plus ultra* of early modern European falconry, and to secure them, peregrines and gyrfalcons were flown at cranes, herons and kites. These high aerial battles were seen as reflections of human intrigues of political and military strategy and power. Heron hawking was a 'game of state' to George Turberville, and poet William Somerville makes the most of these connotations. In his poem 'Field Sports', he describes an 'aerial fight' between falcon and heron that leaves noble, villager and shepherd boy alike transfixed with 'wild amaze':

> The falcon hov'ring flies
> Balanc'd in Air, and confidently bold
> Hangs o'er him like a Cloud, then aims her Blow
> Full at his destin'd Head. The watchful Hern

A saker falcon chases a houbara bustard across the sandy plains of Baluchistan. Houbaras sometimes evade attacks at close range by squirting droppings at their pursuer.

Shoots from her like a blazing Meteor swift
That gilds the Night, eludes her Talons keen,
And pointed Beak, and gains a Length of Way.
Observe th'attentive croud, all Hearts are fix'd
On this important War, and pleasing Hope
Glows in each Breast. The Vulgar and the Great,
Equally happy how, with Freedom share
The common Joy . . . [7]

Compared to these buoyant, unpredictable and sky-covering pursuits, the *waiting on* flight, a speciality of Western falconry, is an elaborate and formal affair. Here, falcons are trained to *wait on* at a high *pitch*, circling perhaps as high as 1,000 feet above the falconer in expectation that quarry – usually ducks, or gamebirds such as pheasants, partridges or grouse – will be flushed below it. When the game is flushed, the whole point of game hawking becomes apparent: the falcon, espying the quarry, tips over into

A peregrine falcon flying at rooks in a pencil drawing by
Karl Wilhelm Friedrich Bauerle (1831–1912).

The *Haut Vol*, high-altitude flight, was revived in the 19th century by the exclusive Royal Loo Hawking Club, which flew peregrines at herons over the open heaths of the Veluwe region of the Netherlands. The herons were usually released after they had been caught.

a vertical stoop, falling at dramatic speed on an intercepting path towards its prey. The sound of a falcon stooping from a towering pitch across miles of sky can be awe-inspiring: a strange, tearing noise like ripping cloth. As the bird cuts through the air, an adrenalin-filled rush of a kind familiar to airshow or Grand Prix attendees is the inevitable result for the onlooker. 'You *are* the bird,' exclaimed falconer Alva Nye.[8] It seems that the quarry will inevitably be overhauled and killed instantly with a clout of the falcon's foot. But inevitable it is not. Most flights end with the quarry escaping and the falcon returning to the falconer's lure.

The lure – a long cord with a leather pad or a pair of dried wings at one end – is also used to exercise the falcon by getting her to chase it in mid-air. It's a device familiar to readers of *The Taming of the Shrew*, in which many obscure falconry terms are encountered. Shakespeare was writing in falconry's European heyday, a time when its terminology was bewilderingly complex. As in any elite activity, the vocabulary and etiquette of falconry had gatekeeping functions; a proficient command of them attested to one's high social position. Jesuit spy Father Southwell, for example, was exceedingly worried that he would reveal his true identity by forgetting his falconry terms.[9]

There were dedicated terms for falconry furniture, for different flight styles, for every part of the falcon. A hawk's talons were her *pounces*, her toes her *petty singles,* her wings her *sails* and chest-feathers her *mail*. When a falcon sneezed, she *snurted*. Some of these terms are still used by falconers: young falcons are *eyasses* and immature wild falcons *passagers*. When a falcon lands she *pitches*; falcons *mount* into the sky, rather than climb; when they wipe their beaks they *feak* and when they shake themselves they *rouse*.

Their original meanings now obscure, some terms continue in more general use today: when hawks drink, they *bowse* or *booze*.

In a 1940s photograph, the American falconer Steve Gatti exercises his peregrine to the lure.

Falconers claim Shakespeare as one of their own. This engraving from J. E. Harting's 1864 *Ornithology of Shakespeare* playfully adds a falcon to the famous Chandos portrait.

Tid-bits are scraps of meat proffered to a falcon; a *cadge* is a field-perch; a *haggard* is a wild adult falcon and thus difficult to train. And while the term might be more familiarly applied to exclusive, eye-wideningly expensive properties in central London, *mews* were originally built to house birds of prey while they moulted in the summer months.

FALCONRY FURNITURE

Despite the arcane terminology of falconry, its equipment, or *furniture*, is relatively simple and eminently practical. Perhaps the most familiar of all is the thin leather *hood*. Popped over the falcon's head it blocks out all light, and apart from its role in the hunting field, its judicious use keeps half-trained or highly strung birds from alarming sights. Hoods come in many designs

– Indian goatskin hoods; soft Arab hoods; stiff, heavy Dutch hoods with coloured side-panels and a wool and feather plume. Modern artisan-falconers have created moulded and beautifully finished hybrid designs that are far lighter and more comfortable for the falcon than many of the ornamented older styles.

Falcons are normally held on the leather-gloved left fist. Arab falconers carry them on a woven *mangalah*, or cuff. The reasons for holding falcons on the left fist are obscure. Medieval clerics unsurprisingly saw it has having mystical significance. According to one manuscript, falcons are carried on the left hand in order that they should fly to the right to seek their prey:

> the left represents temporal things, the right everything that is eternal. On the left sit those who rule over temporal things; all those who in the depths of their hearts desire eternal things fly to the right. There the hawk will catch the dove; that is, he who turns towards the good will receive the grace of the Holy Spirit.[10]

The trailing leg-straps by which the falconer holds the falcon are called *sabq* in Arabic, and are made of plaited silk or cord. Their Western equivalents, *jesses*, are made of soft leather. At home their ends are attached to a metal swivel to stop them twisting, and the swivel in turn to a leash. This leash is tied to a perch or *block* using the falconer's knot – for obvious reasons easily tied and untied with one hand.

For centuries, small silver or brass bells attached to the falcon's legs or tail have been used to locate the falcon while out hawking, their plangent tones audible for half a mile or more downwind. In the 1970s American falconer-engineers developed a tiny radio transmitter that could be attached to a falcon's tail

A plate from Diderot and d'Alembert's 1751 *Encyclopédie* showing the mews (above) and falconry equipment (below): a screen perch, two Dutch hoods, a rufter hood, turf blocks and a cadge for carrying falcons into the field.

or leg. With a range of scores of miles, telemetry systems have dramatically reduced the possibility of losing a falcon. Telemetry was greeted with enthusiasm by falconers in the Gulf States, for whom falconry continues to be a vibrant and popular cultural practice. Conversely, many European falconers viewed this new invention with distaste. A minority pursuit compared to more modern hunting methods, European falconers have tended to validate and define falconry in terms of its rich cultural tradition and long history. They commonly assert historical precedent as a legitimating device, and threats to its established, traditional modes of practice tend to be perceived as a threat to falconry itself. Yet these anti-modernist misgivings seem to have been largely overcome. Today many falcons are flown with a modern radio transmitter attached almost invisibly to the tail – often right next to a Lahore brass bell, manufactured in Pakistan to a design of immense antiquity. *Plus ça change.*

In the United Arab Emirates, falconer Khameez calms a young falcon in training as he picks it up from its *wakr*, or perch.

The falconer's first impression of a new falcon, sitting hooded on her perch, is one of unalloyed wildness. The slightest touch or sound and she'll puff out her feathers and hiss like a snake. Falcons are trained entirely through positive reinforcement. They must never be punished; as solitary creatures, they fail to understand hierarchical dominance relations familiar to social creatures such as dogs or horses. As Lord Tweedsmuir wrote in the 1950s, secure in his impression that falcons were an avian aristocracy:

> No hawk regards you as a master. At the best, they regard you as an ally, who will provide for them and care for them and introduce them to some good hunting. You only have to look at the proud, imperious face of a peregrine falcon to realise that. In reality you become their slave.[11]

Despite Tweedsmuir's characterization of the falcon as a death-dealing dominatrix, falcons can become rather affectionate. In the Gulf States, some falcons jump from their indoor perches and run to the falconer should he call their names. British falconer and author Philip Glasier had a tiercel peregrine that slept on his bookshelf and jumped onto his bed in the morning to wake him by nibbling his ear; another British falconer, Frank Illingworth, had a peregrine that took rides around the garden on the back of his dog; gyrfalcons enjoy playing with tennis balls and footballs.

So how does one train a falcon? Early modern authors capture the key perfectly. Through the falconer's constant attention to the bird's 'stomacke': that is, her appetite and physical condition.

Knight with a falcon, from a 15th-century copy of the Codex Capodilista, tempera on vellum.

Indeed, in the most basic sense, falcons are trained through their stomachs – through associating the falconer with food. If a falcon isn't hungry, is *too high*, she'll see little point either in chasing quarry or returning to the falconer. Conversely, should she be a little *too* thin, or *low* in condition, she'll lack the energy to give that palpable sense of inner urgency in flight that is the watchword of truly exciting falconry. The conditioning of a falcon revolves around a terrifying number of variables: the weather, the time of year, the stage in training, the type of food the falcon has eaten and how much exercise she has had. Falconers assess condition in a variety of ways. Some are quantitative: daily weighing, for example. Others involve tacit knowledges built from years of experience: feeling the amount of muscle around a falcon's breastbone, the bird's posture and demeanour, the way she carries her feathers, even the expression on her face.

Taming and training a falcon is a serious and skilled business. Every autumn, falconers bring new falcons to their sheikhs and princes in the Gulf States. In long meetings, the quality and condition of each falcon are assessed, appraised and measured with fine exactitude. Falcons are tamed rapidly in this falconry culture; they are kept constantly on their falconer's fist, or on perches nearby, totally immersed in everyday human life. While initially stressful, this method quickly promotes an unflappable tameness in the falcon. A similar method, termed 'waking', was commonplace in early modern Europe: the new falcon was kept constantly on someone's fist until it overcame its fears sufficiently to sleep.

Western falcon training today is a far slower process. The untamed falcon is initially handled only while the falconer offers her food on the fist. Soon she associates the falconer with food and jumps to the fist from her perch. The distance she jumps for

Highly ornate lures and hoods from the court of the Holy Roman Emperor Maximilian I (*r.* 1493–1519).

food is gradually extended and she soon flies to the falconer – first on a light line known as a *creance* and then free. In both Arab and Western falconry, free-flying falcons are trained to return to a lure, but more creative methods of retrieving falcons have existed: falconer Roger Upton recounts a story from the days when the only lights in the Saudi desert were campfires. Back then, one Bedouin falconer made sure he only ever fed his falcon right next to the fire. When this falcon became lost during hawking expeditions, she flew back, even at night, to the huge fire her anxious falconer built as a beacon for her return. Every spring he released her in the Hejaz mountains so she could breed, and every October he returned to the mountains, built a big fire and re-trapped her.

'NOTHING SO FREQUENT'

For more than 500 years, falconry was immensely popular across Europe, Asia and the Arab world. It carried enormous cultural capital. Historian Robin Oggins describes early modern European falconry as an almost perfect example of conspicuous consumption; 'expensive, time consuming and useless, and in all three respects [serving] to set its practitioners apart as a class'.[12] Expensive it was. Extraordinarily so. In thirteenth-century England a falcon could cost as much as half the yearly income of a knight. Four hundred years later, Robert Burton maintained that there was 'nothing so frequent' as falconry, that 'he is nobody, that in the season hath not a hawk on his fist. A great art, and many books written on it.'[13] Some European gentlemen hawked every day, even on campaign or when conducting official business. Henry VIII hawked both morning and afternoon if the weather was fine, and would have drowned in a bog while out hawking had his falconer not pulled him out. Medieval Spanish falconer Pero López de Ayala considered falconry an essential part of a princely education, for it prevented sickness and damnation and demanded patience, endurance and skill. For much of its long European history, falconry was considered to exemplify youth and the active life, and, like all elite pursuits, it was ripe for satire. In his 1517 work *De fructu qui ex doctrina percipitur*, the Tudor diplomat and man of letters Richard Pace put these words into the mouth of a nobleman: 'It becomes the sons of gentlemen to blow the horn nicely, to hunt skilfully and elegantly carry and train a hawk! But the study of letters should be left to the sons of rustics.'[14]

Despite falconry's opposition to the *via contemplativa*, clergy were keen falconers too. D'Arcussia suggested that 'more devout souls' should go hawking in order to raise spirits 'brought down from previous vigour by continual study or by having too many concerns.'[15] The councils of 506, 507 and 518 strictly forbade priests and bishops to practise falconry, but the clergy deliberately misinterpreted the word *devots* (devotees) so that the term would not apply to them. Pope Leo X was such an inveterate falconer that he would hawk in any weather. D'Arcussia described him as 'so sharp . . . a sportsman that he would not spare from his wrath anyone . . . who failed to observe any of the duties of Falconry.'[16] William of Wykeham, Bishop of Winchester, complained that nuns taking their falcons into chapel with them interfered with the service, and it's said that an enraged medieval bishop of Ely stormed back into the cathedral and threatened to excommunicate the culprit after he discovered his falcons had been stolen from the vestry.

Holy Roman Emperor Frederick II of Hohenstaufen infamously led a Holy Crusade even after he'd been excommunicated. His contemporaries called him *stupor mundi*, the wonder of the world. Modern falconers know him familiarly as 'Fred the second', consider him the world's greatest-ever falconer and still glean his massive thirteenth-century work *De arte venandi cum avibus*, 'On the art of hunting with birds', for practical hints. Eastern falconry techniques and technologies were imported into Europe through his court; his interpreter Theodore of Antioch translated Arab and Persian falconry works into Latin, and the emperor employed Arab, English, Spanish, German and Italian falconers 'at great expense'. He wrote:

> We . . . summoned from the four corners of the earth masters in the practice of the art of falconry. We entertained these experts in our domains, meantime seeking their opinions, weighting the importance of their knowledge, and endeavouring to retain in memory the more valuable of their words and deeds.[17]

Falconry techniques and knowledges have been traded between disparate cultures for millennia. European knights took falcons with them on the Crusades, and learned how to hood falcons from their foes. In the early twelfth century, in what is now Syria, falconer Usamah Ibn-Muquidh complained that because his hunting land was now adjacent to Frankish territory, his falconry expeditions needed extra horses, attendants and weapons. Falconry's symbolic system was largely shared between both sides, and so it was able to articulate power-struggles and conflicts in

A 19th-century rendering of Emperor Frederick II of Hohenstaufen
(r. 1215–50) and one of his falconers.

ways immediately comprehensible to either. A besieged Richard
I sent an envoy to Saladin to request food for his starving falcons;
Saladin immediately delivered baskets of his best poultry for the
falcons alone. During the siege of Acre in 1190 a prized gyrfalcon
belonging to King Philip I broke its leash and flew straight to the
top of the city walls. Philip was horrified. An envoy requesting
that the falcon be returned was refused, as was a second envoy
accompanied by trumpets, ensigns and heralds, offering 1,000
gold crowns to Saladin in exchange for the errant falcon.

Throughout the early modern period, travelling European
merchants and diplomats encountered falconry traditions that

awed and bewildered them. Marco Polo was familiar with falconry, but its scale in Central Asia astonished him. With bated pen he explained that the falconry expeditions of the Great Khan involved a retinue of ten thousand falconers – a figure not to be taken literally, but surely indicating a sizeable army. On hawking expeditions the Great Khan was borne by up to four elephants. On their backs stood a pavilion furnished inside with gold braided cloth and outside with lion's skins. 'Such facilities', he wrote, 'are required by the Kublai Khan on these hunting excursions also, since he is very much bothered by gout in the feet':

> In this pavilion he always has with him twelve of the best gyrfalcons and twelve of his particularly beloved honour bearers for diversion and for company. The riders beside the Khan inform him when in the vicinity of cranes or other birds flying by. He then raises the curtain of the pavilion, and when he has seen the game, he casts the falcons, which hunt the cranes and overcome them after a long flight. The Khan lies on a comfortable lounge, and the sight of this gives him, as well as the gentlemen serving him and the riders surrounding him, great pleasure.[18]

Persian kings were so enamoured of falconry that they trained sparrows and starlings to catch butterflies, recorded Sir Richard Burton. In the late seventeenth century, English traveller Sir John Chardin enthused about the ability of Persian falconers. One could see them 'all year round in the City and the Country . . . going backwards and forward with a Hawk on their Hand'. Chardin heard of some stranger and less sociable traditions here. It seemed that falcons were once commonly taught to assault men. 'They say', he wrote in wonderment, 'that there are still such Birds in the King's Bird-House. I have not seen any of them, but I hear'd that Aly-couly-can, Governour of Tauris, whom I was particularly acquainted with, could not forbear diverting himself with that dangerous and cruel sport, tho' with the loss of his friends.'[19]

And falconry's reach was extraordinary. In the sixteenth and seventeenth centuries, falcon-traders brought falcons to the French court from Flanders, Germany, Russia, Switzerland, Norway, Sicily, Corsica, Sardinia, the Balearic Islands, Spain,

A late 15th-century gouache of a mounted
falconer with white gyrfalcon.

Turkey, Alexandria, the Barbary States and India. The fifth Earl of Bedford imported hawks from as far afield as North Africa, Nova Scotia and New England. In many European countries only noblemen were allowed to use native falcons. In sixteenth-century England, a thriving smuggling trade developed after foreign hawks were classed as luxuries and were subject to an import duty of a shilling in the pound.

But by the end of the seventeenth century, falconry's popularity was waning in Europe. Louis XIII was exceptional: so obsessed with falconry that he hawked most days of the week, he even composed a libretto for his ballet *La Merlaison* describing the delights of hawking for blackbirds and thrushes. The use of falcons as diplomatic gifts gradually faded in the eighteenth century, and falconry's connection with royalty and nobility won it no favours after the French Revolution. Landowners converted their mews to other uses; new sports had become fashionable: shooting, fox-hunting and horse-racing. By the nineteenth century European falconry had become the pursuit of a very few individuals who had banded together into falconry clubs – and of eccentrics, among whom was Henri de Toulouse-Lautrec's father. Toulouse-Lautrec senior used to walk about the streets of Albi with shirt-tails flapping and falcon on his fist. 'Not wishing, doubtless, to deprive his raptors of the succour of religion', wrote Henri, 'he would give them holy water to drink.'[20]

IMPERIAL FALCONRY

But falconry was still practised elsewhere. In 1913 the American writer William Coffin explained that while in Europe 'it exists ... only as a fad of a few medieval-minded sportsmen, in the East, where the art of falconry perhaps originated, it flourishes still.'[21]

Algerian falconers setting out for the field. Romantic, orientalist representations of falconry were commonplace in the late 19th century, and this 1898 painting by Gustave Henri Marchetti is a prime example.

Nineteenth- and early twentieth-century writers often used falconry's persistence in non-Western cultures as evidence that such cultures either lagged far behind the West or, indeed, existed entirely outside the progress of history. And falconry had further roles to play in the age of Empire. Still the sport of elite or ruling classes in many countries, it seemed to offer a global naturalization of social hierarchy. Hunting-crazy officers in nineteenth-century British India took up falconry and employed local falconers. Not only did they enjoy the sport, but they saw it as a means of reinforcing their elite social status and winning loyalty from Indian soldiers under their command. In the North Punjab the Regiment of Guides (Cavalry and Infantry) kept a regimental establishment of saker falcons; officers flew them at ravine deer and houbara.[22] Lieut. Col. E. Delmé-Radcliffe of the 88th Connaught Rangers famously responded to the first cries of his newborn child with the exclamation 'Good God! There's a *cat* at my falcons!'[23] Lieut. Col. E. H. Cobb took up hawking while political agent in Gilgit in the 1940s because a shortage of shotgun cartridges precluded partridge shooting. But to his delight he soon discovered that in falconry at least 'the local Chiefs readily supported the British Officers'.[24] 'From time immemorial', he wrote happily, falconry 'has been considered to be a princely sport and nowhere can it be practised to such advantage as by the feudal chieftains of the Hindu Kush . . . for they have the power to control large areas of falconry ideally suited to falconry and also to command a large army of falconers.' He added that as far as falconry goes, 'the Asiatic methods are very similar to our own'.[25]

These imperial imaginings typically obliterated any drive to understand how falconry's social functions differed across cultures. Such blindness is still encountered. Even today one encounters explanations of the rise of falconry in the Arabian Gulf as being a means for nomadic people to obtain additional protein to supplement a meagre diet. This functional explanation is as blind to cultural nuance as that of many a nineteenth-century commentator. For falconry has always had significant

Bedouin men hawking on horse-back with saker and lanner falcons, Palestine, between 1900 and 1920.

spiritual and social importance in Bedouin culture, where it is highly valued for its egalitarian nature and the qualities of self-denial and generosity it fosters. A hawking expedition grants falconers of all social backgrounds space to meet as equals in the desert, to swap stories and share food, while their falcons doze in the firelight.

THE FALCON GENTLE

We learn that spy-hero Richard Hannay's son is a falconer in John Buchan's thriller *Island of Sheep*. 'If you keep hawks,' Buchan explains, 'you have to be a pretty efficient nursemaid, and feed them and wash them and mend for them.'[26] Indeed. Falconry granted the English gentleman a legitimate form of domesticity: when attending to a falcon, one could be both manly *and* a nursemaid. Falcon-training mirrored the education of the public schoolboy, the purpose of which was to tame and control the natural strength, wildness and unruliness of the growing boy through discipline, physical restraint, self-sacrifice, *virtu* and honour. And so with the falcon. For centuries, the process of training a falcon has been seen as training oneself, learning patience and bodily and emotional self-control. 'Training a falcon trains the man quite as much as the man trains the falcon,' explained Harold Webster succinctly in 1964,[27] a notion that perhaps informs programmes at several British prisons where inmates keep and breed falcons and hawks.

The notion that the emasculating effects of modern life can be cured by contact with wild nature has been a standard trope in writings on masculinity from Roosevelt to Robert Bly. Associating with wild or ferocious animals – through hunting them or, in the case of falconry, training them – has often been cast as a panacea for such lily-livery. In this tradition, through training a falcon the falconer assumes some of the wildness of the falcon, whilst the falcon correspondingly assumes the manners of a man. 'One never really tames a falcon,' wrote one American falconer in the 1950s. 'One just becomes a little wild like she is.'[28] Masculine qualities considered lost or marginalized in modern life – wildness, power, strength and so on – had already been projected onto falcons. Through the psychologically charged identifications of trainer and hawk during the training process the falconer can repossess these qualities while the falcon at the same time becomes 'civilized'. No wonder there are still so few female falconers.

T. H. White clearly saw magical, almost Freudian transferences between human and hawk as intrinsic to falconry. He described his own attempts as the project of a man 'alone in a wood, being tired of most humans in any case, to train a person who was not human, but a bird'.[29] White decided to 'wake' his hawk by the old-fashioned method. This involved 'reciting Shakespeare to keep the hawk awake and thinking with pride and happiness about the hawk's tradition':

There was a bas-relief of a Babylonian with a hawk on his fist in Khorsabad, which dated from about 3,000 years ago. Many people were not able to understand why this was pleasant, but it was. I thought it was right that I should now be happy to continue as one of a long line. The unconscious of the race was a medium in which one's own unconscious microscopically swam, and not only in that of the living race but of all the races which had gone before. The Assyrian had begotten children. I grasped that ancestor's bony hand, in which all the knuckles were as well defined as the nutty calf of his bas-relief leg, across the centuries.[30]

Many twentieth-century commentators shared White's desire for historical continuity and community; they also saw falconry as a romantic, pastoralist, anti-modern pursuit. In 1930s America, an era of chivalric youth groups such as the Knights of King Arthur, many boys caught the falconry bug because they were beguiled by falconry's fantasies of reliving a knightly past. Grown-ups were not immune. Arch-ruralist J. Wentworth Day's account of a day's hawking with the British Falconers Club in Kent explained how the hawking expedition was a trip to a lost past:

standing on the hump-backed vallum of a British earth-work, all the sea and the marshes at your feet, the wind in your face, the hawk on your fist, you may know that you are, for a brief space, a heir of the ages. A minor page of history has turned back a thousand years.[31]

On the left, the novelist John Buchan holds up a kestrel; on the right, his son has a goshawk. Buchan senior was for some years the president of the Oxford University Falconry Club.

The notion that falconry could be a kind of virtual time-travelling is commonplace in inter-war writings on the sport. After the horrors of the Great War, falconry allowed one to reclaim historical continuity; it was a bond, a healing link with a lost pastoral age. Falconers themselves rarely wrote in such purple prose. They tended to keep any lyrical sentiments hidden beneath the bluff demeanour of the practised field-sportsman. But they too were at pains to point out that British falconry had never died out and had an unbroken link with the past.

Fifty years later, the final passages of Stephen Bodio's book *A Rage for Falcons* seem cast in the same mould. Describing a group of modern American falconers attending to hawk and quarry in the snow, Bodio muses that 'there is no way to tell where or when this picture comes from, not on three continents, not in four thousand years.'[32] But falconry is not all history for Bodio. Like many modern falconers, he values falconry's ability to reforge

A 19th-century bas-relief of the Shah of Persia, Nâser al-Din (d. 1896).

'Shakespeare meets Abercrombie and Fitch': post-war America
reinvents falconry.

links with nature. 'Here right at the very edge of the city,' runs
the book's final sentence, 'it seems we have found a way of going
on, of touching the wild in this twentieth century.' His view is
analogous to that of Professor Tom Cade, who describes falconry

as a form of high-intensity birdwatching. Bodio characterizes falconers as having 'a feeling for the woods and fields, an intuitive grasp of ecology'.[33] This notion of falconer-as-ecologist was first championed by Aldo Leopold in the 1940s. For him, falconry was superior to modern, technologically augmented hunting methods. It provided insight into the workings of ecological processes, demanded strenuous outdoor activity and required the learning of many practical skills. At heart, it taught the falconer a fortuitous psychological ability: to maintain the correct balance between wild and civilized states – in both falcon and falconer. 'At the slightest error in the technique of handling,' Leopold wrote, 'the falconer's hawk may either "go tame" like *Homo sapiens* or fly away into the blue. All in all falconry is the perfect hobby.'[34]

THE FORGOTTEN FIELD SPORT?

Yet many would disagree with Leopold, seeing falconry less as a means of recapturing right relations with nature, and more as a bloodthirsty, atavistic activity. The RSPCA lamented the irrevocable coarsening of the minds and manners of young ladies who took up the sport in the nineteenth century. A century later, one British anti-hunting group explained that falconers fly their falcons in remote countryside in order to prevent members of the public seeing what they are doing. I still recall the raised eyebrow and acid response of one falconer to this statement: 'Do birdwatchers go to remote places so that no one can see them watching birds?' he enquired.

Falconry's position within the highly polarized hunting debate is intriguing. Its opponents describe it as the 'forgotten' field sport, for it seems aligned with bird-watching rather than hunting in

An anti-falconry engraving from a 19th-century publication by the Royal Society for the Prevention of Cruelty to Animals. Note the entirely imaginary dramatic elements here: the live bird on a string and the bow tied around a falcon.

today's cultural milieu: falconry books, for example, tend to be shelved in the natural-history section of British bookshops rather than in the hunting section. Falconer-biologist Nick Fox enthusiastically promotes falconry as a 'green' activity, arguing that the falconer 'doesn't need to modify the countryside by building sports grounds or golf courses, or by killing vermin, rearing large numbers of game birds, and restricting public access . . . falconry is a natural, low-impact field-sport, self-sustaining and well-suited to the needs of modern man'.[35] His position is shared by at least one academic ornithologist who told me that good falconry is a particularly enlightened form of animal–human relationship, so perfectly does it match the behavioural repertoire of the wild animal.

Yet as he pointed out, larger problems quite unrelated to one's moral stance on hunting are associated with falconry. Perhaps

Falconry as a symbol of Arab cultural identity meets Bald Eagle as a symbol of American imperialism: a 2004 cartoon from Al Jazeera.

the best known is that of the illegal taking of young falcons from the wild. Thieves exerted a serious toll on European falcon eyries in the 1960s and '70s. Along with the activities of egg-collectors, these depredations exerted considerable pressure on populations threatened by pesticides. Today, with captive-bred birds readily available, eyrie thefts are thankfully much rarer in Europe; offenders are treated harshly by conservation organizations, falconry organizations and the law alike. But sadly, this is far from being true elsewhere. Falcon smuggling, sometimes small-scale, sometimes large and mafia-run, has had devastating effects on some saker populations in the former Soviet Union. At the same time, falconers were directly responsible for one of the most successful feats of conservation ever undertaken: the restoration of the peregrine falcon to much of the United States in the 1970s. The story of the decline and recovery of the peregrine falcon is truly extra-ordinary. Thirty years ago, doomy predictions of the species' extinction were common. Now the peregrine has been removed from the American Endangered Species list. Millions of dollars, thousands of people, universities, governments, corporations, even the military, were involved in its restoration. What makes such conservation success stories so compelling, so mesmerizing?

four
Threatened Falcons

SNOW LEOPARDS. Giant pandas. Peregrine falcons. Bengal tigers. All are rare and spectacular animals, icons of environmentalism, stars of the small screen. Their faces are familiar from magazine covers and their lives are favoured subjects for nature writers. These are species bathed in an aura denied other, commoner creatures. Put bluntly, they're celebrities. They exist in the wild, but they live in glossy magazines. And the peregrine is right up there on the 'A-list', along with a select few other icons of extinction. Rarity is a slippery concept. Separating its biological from its cultural meanings is a difficult task. Animals on that A-list seem made of rarity, an identity-characteristic almost impossible to 'think round' to get to the animal itself. Just as the decline in house sparrows in Britain in the 1990s was masked by the species' presumed ubiquity, so upturns in the fortune of celebrity endangered animals often fail to register on popular consciousness. In 2004, for example, a BBC webpage described peregrine falcons as being 'now rare enough to share the same protection as the Giant Panda', even though peregrines are commoner today in Britain than ever before.[1]

How does one become a celebrity animal? Both pandas and peregrines got their A-list status during the 1960s and '70s. Pandas sent as diplomatic gifts from China were Cold War icons; their sex lives in Western zoos had ramifications far beyond their

Traders selling saker falcons in Beijing, 1909. These may have been destined for falconry, but, despite government protection, falcons are still eaten in parts of China.

conservation value. And peregrines? The threat to the peregrine in the 1950s and '60s was real. An entire race of peregrines – the huge, dark *anatum* birds of the eastern US – became extinct and across a vast swathe of North America and Europe peregrine populations plummeted to frighteningly low levels. This disaster mightily increased a series of symbolic attributions previously accorded peregrines – ones relating to wilderness and primitivist glamour – and transformed the peregrine falcon into a supreme icon of environmental destruction, a symbol of how science and technological progress had betrayed its promise to build a better world.

PARADISE LOST

Part of the compulsion of the falcon conservation story as it is generally told is derived from its mythical structure. It's a familiar one – a biblical one. Once, in a distant, Edenic past, it explains, humans lived in harmony with falcons, accorded them reverence. They were worshipped as gods or messengers to the gods. Later, they were treasured as falconry birds, the consorts of kings and emperors. Then came the Fall. Our bond with the wild was lost, and the downturn in the symbolic and biological fortunes of falcons was vast and desperate, first with the massive nineteenth-century raptor extermination campaigns, and second with the calamitous effects of pesticides on falcons in the 1950s and '60s. But this is an Edenic story with an upside, of course, for we are telling it to ourselves: enlightenment and redemption have already occurred. A gradual understanding of the importance of these birds to natural ecosystems, coupled with a new attitude towards predators and nature as a whole, drove us to save them in the nick of time. Once again, it seems, humans understand and protect these special birds.

The Eden story is a powerful legitimating myth. It can be a force for good, energizing conservation action and promoting consideration of the ethics of human relations with the natural world. But like all myths it is a partial reading, obscuring facts that get in the way of the story. Falcons were indeed worshipped as manifestations of divinity in ancient Egypt. But the massive trade in live falcons for mummification 'falls out' of the story. In early modern Europe, falcons were certainly the birds of kings. But what of the innumerable falcons that perished as they were shipped across continents by falcon traders? And while falcons were protected by law in the Middle Ages, with harsh punishments for commoners who dared to catch falcons or take their eggs, such laws evidence the exercise of power, not concern for the welfare of falcons. We should be wary of ascribing an enlightened view of nature to medieval kings simply because they wished to protect their own symbolic capital. And crucially, the Eden myth masks clear and present conservation dangers. It would be crazy not to celebrate the return of the peregrine falcon after the dark DDT era, or fail to applaud the passionate hard work of those individuals and institutions that helped this happen. But delight should be tempered with a realization that we are not wholly redeemed; this is not the end of the story; habitat loss, pesticides and falcon smuggling are still endangering falcon populations across much of the world, as the end of this chapter shows.

But the Edenic mythical structure of the falcon story is, however, rooted in historical reality. This story can only be told at all because the cultural history of falcons has been indubitably marked by spectacular, vast changes in their symbolic fortunes.

THE FALL

By the nineteenth century, shooting held the sporting capital once accorded to falconry. 'Shooting flying' had become the test of the true marksman, the pursuit of elite sporting society. Shotgun retorts, not falcon bells, rang across European moor, crag and manor. Estate owners competed with each other to provide record bags of game for invited guns. And any animals that threatened to compete with guns for game were *persona non grata*. No longer the consorts of kings, falcons had become the worst of vermin. And so began an era of vast raptor extermination campaigns:

> Sportsmen early learn that this hawk is exceptionally obnoxious to the amusement . . . it is a remorseless marauder and murderer, killing for amusement after satisfying its hunger completely. No man should be accounted a genuine sportsman with the gun who does not instantly slaughter the Duck Hawk [peregrine] on sight.[2]

Killing birds of prey was a condition of employment for nine-teenth-century British gamekeepers. On one Scottish estate, for example, new keepers signed an oath that they would use their 'best endeavours to destroy all birds of prey, etc., with their nests, wherever they can be found therein. So help me God.'[3] Fallen falcon corpses were hung on gibbets, or sent to taxidermists who transformed them into trophies for display in domestic spaces: the bird of kings reduced to a bundle of bones and feathers swing-ing from a tree, or cured with arsenic and set behind glass. 'Alas!', wrote British falconer-naturalist J. E. Harting in his 1871 guide *The Ornithology of Shakespeare*, 'that we should live to see our noble falcons gibbeted, like thieves, upon the "keeper's tree".'[4]

A few balked at the slaughter. Scottish keeper Dugald Macintyre was, unusually, a falconer; he saw falcons as natural sportsmen sharing the skills, mores and spoils of his world. Wild peregrines, he explained, timed their stoops at quarry 'just as a great shot times the arrival of his shot-charge at a distant flying target',[5] and he thought they dispatched grouse far more

A recently mounted peregrine falcon, from Montagu Browne's 1884 *Practical Taxidermy*. The cords, cards and pins were removed after a few weeks.

humanely than humans. But viewing falcons as natural sports-men didn't preclude their killing. In many cases, it simply made them a more tempting target for the nineteenth-century sporting gentleman. Shooting a falcon granted him an opportunity to pit his wits against an opponent that possessed sufficient common-alities with his own self-image to make the battle a worthy one. A duel, say. A shot peregrine sent to Roland Ward, taxidermist of Piccadilly, and then displayed in one's house, was at once a trophy, a guarantor of one's prowess and a metaphorical extension of oneself. The imperilled peregrines of Henry Williamson's 1923 nature-fable *The Peregrine's Saga* clearly demonstrate this con-tinuing alignment of falcon with modern aristocrat. Williamson's peregrines are mirror images of a fading British aristocracy dealt a double blow by the First World War and harsh new tax regi-mens. Blood-lineages, power, history and nobility are what Williamson's peregrines are made of: one peregrine family, 'the Devon Chakcheks', was 'a family haughtier and more feared than any other in the West Country'; an 'ancient and noble house'.[6] Indeed, an 'English King' had once conferred an earldom on an ancestor of one of Williamson's falcons.[7]

In the 1900s US Government scientists showed that not all raptors were game-bird slaughterers; some preferred to eat mice and frogs. Raptors could now be seen as either beneficial or per-nicious, as having 'good or bad habits'. Depression-era bird enthusiasts seized upon this with glee. They circulated leaflets that described hawks as 'soldiers' waging war against enemy rodents that ate American crops. 'Protecting hawks', they wrote, 'will help prevent starvation'.[8] But the peregrine's American common name of 'Duck Hawk' won it no favours from hunters in this period, however, and nor did the large falcons gain much from the results of economic ornithologist's examinations:

Gray Gyrfalcon (*Falco rusticolus rusticolus*); 5 stomachs; 4 contained field mice; the other, remains of a Gull. Prairie falcon (*F. mexicanus*); good and bad habits about balanced; takes game birds and also pernicious rodents . . . Duck Hawk (*F. peregrinus*); harmful to water birds and poultry; takes also small birds; feeds to some extent on insects and mice but on the whole more harmful than useful.[9]

Killing 'bad' birds of prey was considered a morally and biologically responsible act. The view was to persist well into the twentieth century. America's foremost bird conservation organization, the Audubon Society, shot birds of prey on their bird sanctuaries in the 1920s; in many European countries, bounties were still paid for dead raptors in the 1950s and '60s. Conservation's roots in game management were reflected in the policy of many organizations and governmental bodies. In 1958 a delegate at the International Union for the Conservation of Nature told Phyllis Barclay-Smith that she couldn't be a bird preservationist if she advocated the protection of birds of prey.

THE ENLIGHTENMENT?

Halcyon days were had by hawk-shooters in interwar America. So many of them congregated to shoot migrating raptors from Blue Mountain in Pennsylvania that their spent brass shells were collected and sold for scrap. But times were changing. Alerted by horrified bird lovers, Rosalie Edge bought the mountain in 1934, renamed it Hawk Mountain, and ushered in a new era; crowds now came to watch raptors, not kill them. In Massachusetts, ornithologist Joseph Hagar posted hawk wardens to guard each peregrine eyrie from egg collectors, gunners, falconers and other disturbances. Watching peregrine eyries brought other benefits, too: sublime sights of flying skills surpassing those of the world's greatest aviators; Hagar's excitement at the spectacle of one 'diving, plunging, saw-toothing' displaying tiercel peregrine is palpable. The tiercel 'fell like a thunderbolt . . . described three, successive, vertical loop-the-loops' and then

roared out over our heads with the wind rushing through his wings like ripping canvas. Against the background of the cliff his terrific speed was much more apparent than it had been in the open sky. The sheer excitement of watching such a performance was tremendous; we felt a strong impulse to stand and cheer.[10]

Ornithologists Roger Tory Peterson and Richard Herbert at a Hudson River peregrine eyrie in 1948. Recreational egg-collecting took its toll on more accessible falcon nests in the early 20th century. Thankfully the practice is now far less common.

Hagar's passage hints also at another changing symbolic milieu for falcons. The 'ripping canvas' is a clue: the passage is drenched in the language of air-age evangelism. Falcons were symbolically made anew by the craze for aviation and its themes of aerial heroism, wind, speed and power that swept the nation in the inter-war years.

Surges of environmental nationalism, spurred in part by increasing tourism, were increasingly promoting animal species as living examples of America's wild past.[11] Animals were now serious entertainment, 'stories' of American history to be read by the citizen. Field ornithologist Arthur Allen pleaded for mercy for the peregrine by writing a 'bird-biography' in a young person's bird-study magazine that presented the peregrine in terms of a thrillingly romantic primitivism. He wrote it in the voice of the peregrine – the voice of a thousand boy's adventure magazines.

> I and my story are not for the faint hearted . . . let me arouse in you only those feelings known to the savage breast: the joy of physical combat, the thrill at physical destruction and the fall of the adversary. Let me but give you one *elemental* thrill, and I have done for you that in which all the lesser feathered folk have failed and I am satisfied.[12]

Absorbing such wonderfully primitive falcon qualities no longer necessitated shooting them. Now you could 'capture' them on camera, or commune with them through telescopes or binoculars. Or through training them: falconry had a strong renaissance in this period. The films, lectures, books and articles of Captain C.W.R. Knight revealed a very different kind of falcon. Knight was a hugely popular lecturer of the period; falconer, talented filmmaker, dedicated naturalist, raconteur and natural showman, his stage appearances with his trained golden eagle Mr Ramshaw in the US and UK were legendary. Knight promoted falcons as swashbuckling adventurers, yes, and brave fighters, but also good mothers and fathers. These falcons weren't villains: they were model citizens.

Energetic young falconer-naturalist twins Frank and John Craighead built on Knight's legacy with a series of popular books and photo-essays. They saw their own adventurous selves mirrored in the falcons they studied. Here, Frank Craighead exchanges looks with a wild female peregrine:

> Those eyes revealed her nature, and in them I could see her life. I could see love of freedom, of wild unconfined spaces. I could see the spirit of adventure, the desire for thrills, an appetite for daring. I could see the roving, wandering lust of a Ulysses of the air, a vagabond that was out to see the world and to challenge it.[13]

The Craighead twins described their trained raptors in terms previously reserved for traditional family pets; these falcons were loveable, characterful birds. The 'gentle intelligent look [of] recognition and friendliness' of their young peregrine, Ulysses, changed for the better as he grew into adulthood, his puppy-like curiosity maturing into a powerful independence and reserve: witness here how the falcon traces the culturally sanctioned trajectory of American youth.[14]

The Craigheads themselves matured; years later, in the 1950s, they published a monograph on predation ecology that promoted raptors as guardians of ecological order. Raptor predation balanced prey populations with each other and with their total environment, creating a mean, a middle path. And intriguingly, new, scientific understandings of falcons often coincided with much earlier understandings of their natural roles. Across the Atlantic, ecologist Harry Southern saw a valuable role for raptors in the reconstruction of post-war Britain. 'Carefully contrived introductions' of birds of prey, he suggested, would reduce the populations of rodents that blighted agricultural production and prevented 'the regeneration of our national forests'.[15] For Southern, raptors were allies; scientific co-workers in large-scale ecological experiments for the public good. And just as a well-functioning society was founded on different human roles and professions, contemporary ecologists saw each species as having its own role and profession in the society of nature. And the role of falcons? As 'invulnerable species' at the top of trophic pyramids. This characterization of falcons as top of the food chain, as the terminal focus of energy in a wildlife community, strengthened their long-standing alignment with high social status. The falcon was seen as the romantic 'embodiment of true majesty', but now this familiar notion could be guaranteed by science itself. Such a conflation of ecological theory and popular cultural symbolism appears to have informed the final sentence of Southern's article, in which he proposed that 'vanishing or lost birds of prey should be encouraged to re-enter into their kingdoms'.[16]

EXTINCTION

But falcons were doing precisely the reverse. Quietly, and almost invisibly, they were disappearing. Despondent falcon enthusiasts were the first to note that their local falcons were failing to breed, but had no idea why. Nor did they have any inkling of the wider picture. In Massachusetts, for example, Joseph Hagar

The large, dark, eastern North American *anatum* peregrine. A few years after this photograph was taken, pesticides had wiped out this entire race.

blamed raccoons for the year-on-year failure of his local peregrine eyrie. When the parent birds finally disappeared from their historic cliff in 1950, they left a history of four strange years of sick chicks, shell fragments and vanishing eggs. Across the Atlantic on the rocky, surf-buffeted coast of Cornwall, British peregrine enthusiast Dick Treleaven was similarly puzzled. He reported that only one of six eyries he observed had successfully raised young in 1957 and in 1958 all of them failed. Such ominous reports by amateur naturalists were not so much discounted by mainstream scientists as simply missed. For example, Treleaven reported his findings in *The Falconer*, the journal of the British Falconers Club, a publication outside the purview of academic ornithologists.

And so, in 1963, British ornithologists were stunned when the results of a national population survey of the peregrine were published by Nature Conservancy biologist Derek Ratcliffe.

Ironically, this government survey had been spurred by complaints from racing-pigeon owners that there were too many peregrines in modern Britain. Hardly. The figures were shocking. Britain's peregrine populations were in free-fall: they were less than half of their pre-war level. Only three pairs were left in the whole of southern England. Historic eyries were empty; hardly any young were being reared; and sinister reports were coming in of female peregrines eating their own eggs.

Ratcliffe suspected that pesticides were causing this decline. There had been a public outcry over dramatic kills of farmland birds in the late 1950s and early 1960s, and a new generation of agricultural chemicals were the known culprits. These chemical agents – aldrin, endrin, dieldrin, heptachlor and the US military's wonder-agent, DDT – were being heavily used across agricultural areas of Britain, western Europe and, most heavily of all, in the eastern USA. They were stable compounds that did not break down after they were applied. They persisted, became concentrated in the food chain, gradually building up in the tissues of predators to lethal or sub-lethal levels. The evidence for a

A chillingly jolly and wholly inaccurate early advertisement for DDT.

pesticide-related peregrine decline mounted: Ratcliffe had already found that one addled Scottish peregrine egg contained four different pesticides, including DDE, the breakdown product of DDT. And the peregrine's disappearance could be correlated with agricultural land use: peregrines had declined fastest in arable farming areas, and the speed and spread of the decline seemed to match the pattern of insecticide use in post-war Britain.

The year 1962 saw the publication of Rachel Carson's impassioned exposé of the pesticide industry and its products, *Silent Spring*, an incendiary tract that enraged the chemical industry and alerted a whole generation to the horrors of pollution. In exquisite prose, Carson detailed the new pesticide compounds and their effects on habitats, communities, animals and people. The amount of DDT being used was extraordinary. In eastern US orchards, for example, repeat applications left as much as 32 lb of the stuff per acre. The dark-hooded eastern *anatum* American peregrines that hunted prey over such orchards were hardest hit of all. Their decline in the 1940s and '50s had been unexpected, unprecedented, almost unobserved, and in some areas almost complete. They were soon to be extinct. Environmental journalist David Zimmerman decided later that 'the peregrine declined unnoticed because it is not adorable, a woman's bird, easily kept track of on lawn and feeder – and easily missed. It is a man's bird, a strong, silent, solitary raptor.'[17]

PROOF AND PANIC

As *Silent Spring* hit the bookstands, the eminent American ornithologist Joseph Hickey heard that not a single one of these 'strong and silent' raptors had fledged in the whole eastern US that year. 'I think I assumed', he later said, 'that falconers – real and would-be – had been very, very busy. I did not realise that most of the eyries in this region had by this time been actually and mysteriously deserted.'[18] Alarmed, he organized a peregrine survey and so appalling were the results – all of the hundred or so eyries surveyed were abandoned – that he convened an international conference on the peregrine at the University of Wisconsin–Madison in 1965. The delegates heard news worse than anyone had imagined. As the reports came in, a terrifying picture emerged. This was not a local problem: it was a transcontinental, perhaps global one. It seemed the peregrine might disappear forever.

Derek Ratcliffe's conference presentation was persuasive. It maintained that pesticides had caused this decline. Ratcliffe had also solved the mystery of falcons eating their own eggs. While handling eggshells from a recently deserted British eyrie he noticed that they seemed thinner than those of eggs from old museum collections. Following up his hunch he discovered that modern eggshells were 20 per cent thinner than pre-war shells – thus they were easily crushed during incubation. And once inadvertently broken, female peregrines did what they'd always done with broken eggs – ate them. The same thinning was occurring in US peregrine eggs. And later, two government laboratories, Monks Wood Experimental Station in Britain and the Patuxent Wildlife Research Center in Maryland, finally supplied experimentally tested proof that peregrines were accumulating large loads of DDT in their bodies by preying on contaminated birds. Poisoned peregrines either died outright, or, because the metabolites of DDT affected calcium uptake, they laid thin-shelled, unviable eggs.

As the plight of the peregrine came to the public eye, those old parallels between human and hawk achieved a startling new significance. To a public suffering from extreme Cold War paranoia, a public who had lost trust in technological fixes, lost trust in governments, who had suffered scares over Thalidomide, Strontium-90, fallout, oil spills and nuclear oblivion, pesticides were one more nail in the coffin of institutional science and the myth of progress. The falcon became 'a distilled essence of wildness' as *Defenders of Wildlife* magazine put it.[19]

And it became a human analogue, too. Parallels between radiation sickness and pesticide poisoning were graphically traced: again and again the public stared at neat little pyramidal diagrams showing how radioactive fallout fell onto grass, was eaten by cows, accumulated in their milk and finally ended up sequestered in the bones of nursing mothers. These bioaccumulation diagrams were almost indistinguishable from others showing the build-up of DDT in the tissues of another top predator, the peregrine.

Suddenly, falcon and human were fellow-sufferers of the industrial disease, both at the tops of their respective food chains, and the fate of the peregrine became a parable of the effluent society, an ominous foreshadowing of the fate of mankind itself. Disney's TV nature-biopic *Varda, the Peregrine Falcon* revolved around the 'dark and unhappy environmental threat to the Peregrine's survival' and became the highest-rated show of 1968,

Prime Minister Harold Wilson meets a dead peregrine on a visit to Monks Wood Experimental Research Station, 1970.

with 60 million viewers.[20] British Prime Minister Harold Wilson toured the toxic chemicals unit at Monks Wood Experimental Research Station in 1970 and stared gloomily at a dead peregrine in front of the photographers. The white heat of the technological revolution had had unfortunate side effects.

CLINICAL ORNITHOLOGY

What could be done? Protecting the peregrine was essential – and legislation duly followed. But persecution wasn't the problem. Pesticides were. Many delegates at Hickey's conference wanted to do something *now*. Many were falconers, practically minded obsessives horrified by the possible extinction of the peregrine and aghast that they might never again be able to fly the species.

In Britain, a hard-won voluntary ban on some of the persistent pesticides had been achieved, and the decline of peregrines seemed to have slowed. But in the US things were critical. Thirteen of the Madison conference delegates formed the Raptor Research Foundation under the leadership of falconer Don Hunter. The RRF saw itself as a clearing house to assemble and coordinate information on raptor ecology and captive breeding – at heart, it was a crash programme, an all-out effort to stop the extinction of the peregrine. Its meetings were arduous, intense. They ran from 8 o'clock in the morning until 10.30 at night: passionate brainstorming sessions on possibilities, strategies, techniques.

These individuals pioneered radically manipulative and intrusive conservation techniques far from the 'protect and conserve' ethos of hands-off environmentalists. David Zimmerman described this new applied science as 'clinical ornithology': active human interventions in the life cycles of endangered birds. It was an unremarkable methodology for falconers and aviculturalists familiar with the practical aspects of handling captive birds. So, they thought: why not rescue thin-shelled eggs from eyries and hatch them in artificial incubators, later returning the young to the nest? How about cross-fostering young peregrines into prairie falcon nests for the prairie falcons to rear? Most radical of all, would it be possible to breed falcons in captivity and release the young into a cleaner future wild? These plans required untested skills and techniques. Was it possible to mass-produce falcons in captivity? If so, *how*? Would it work? What did you need?

For many commentators in the early 1970s, mass-producing falcons in captivity was unthinkable. How could one expect a doomed, distilled essence of wildness to breed in a pen like a chicken or pigeon? Faith McNulty wrote in the *New Yorker* that falcon breeding was a feat 'so difficult that it cannot repopulate the wild or provide birds for fanciers'.[21] But she was already being proved wrong. Backyard falcon breeders had taken up the challenge across North America, building a vast assortment of pens and aviaries, and all praying that their peregrines, prairie falcons, lanner falcons and other raptors would breed. These private efforts coexisted with several large institutional projects, the origins of which can all be traced back to that first RRF meeting: a Canadian Wildlife Service facility run by Richard Fyfe in Alberta, California's Santa Cruz Predatory Bird Research Group and the Raptor Research Center at the University of Minnesota.

But whether falcon enthusiasts keeping a pair of falcons in a modified shed or a whole team of PhDs watching peregrines on CCTV, everyone shared data, reports and skills. The question *How does one breed falcons?* was all that mattered. And gradually things became clearer. You didn't need a huge aviary to breed a

Domesticated quail are an excellent food source for captive-bred falcons.
A female peregrine stares down the photographer before feeding her
three young eyasses.

falcon. They liked relatively enclosed aviaries. They liked a choice
of nest-ledges. If you removed a first clutch of eggs for artificial
incubation, the pair would lay another clutch, vastly increasing
their productivity. Young birds taken as nestlings were far more
likely to breed in captivity than birds trapped at a later age. And
so on.

THE PEREGRINE FUND

In the US the falcon-breeding facility at Cornell University
rapidly became the most successful and famous project of all.
It was the brainchild of Tom Cade, Director of the Cornell
Laboratory of Ornithology. Cade had been a falcon aficionado
from the moment he'd watched a female peregrine cut down a
coot over San Dismas Reservoir in California as a boy. 'We heard
a sound, a whistling sound like a six-inch shell passing overhead.
It was a peregrine,' he recalled.[22]

Cornell's 230-foot-long falcon building was so well-appointed that it became known as the Peregrine Palace. It housed 40 pairs of large falcons, largely donated by falconers, in spacious, experimental breeding chambers under constant CCTV surveillance. The project aimed to mass-produce peregrines for falconers, for scientific study and, most crucially, for reintroduction into the wild, and it soon became incorporated as the Peregrine Fund, Inc. This was conservation 'big science', a vigorous, proselytizing effort, and one requiring serious funding. The funds came from diverse sources – the National Science Foundation, IBM, the Audubon Society, World Wildlife Fund, US Fish and Wildlife Service, even the US Army Materiel Command. The Peregrine Fund's proactive attitude to publicity lent it a high media profile and it received thousands of private donations from a concerned and willing public; from the US Army to the proceeds of school-yard and cookie sales, every dollar counted.

By 1973 the Peregrine Fund was producing 20 young from only three fertile pairs of peregrines, and in Alberta Richard Fyfe's project was also producing young – as were many breeders across the US. And Peregrine Fund co-founder Bob Berry had pioneered a new technique to breed even more falcons: artificial insemination. A standard technique for present-day falcon breeders, it requires considerable – and unusual – skills. If a young falcon is reared by humans, it will 'imprint' upon them, responding to them as if they were falcons themselves. The task of an imprint handler is to build a pair-bond with an imprinted falcon, mirroring the behaviour of a real falcon: bowing like a courting falcon, making 'chupping' courtship noises, bringing it food. Eventually the falcon – if male – will mate with its handler, copulating on a specially designed latex hat. The imprint handler then collects the falcon semen with a pipette and uses

Sexually imprinted on humans, this tiercel peregrine is copulating with a specially constructed hat. Beneath the hat is Peregrine Fund falcon breeder Cal Sandfort.

it to inseminate an imprinted female falcon. It's all in a day's work. These bird–human AI relationships tend to evoke mild discomfiture or sniggering from the general public. Imprint handlers soon learn not to discuss the ins and outs of their profession with their non-falcon-breeder friends.

Scientist-conservationists such as Tom Cade and Richard Fyfe fascinated the media. Lacking falcon obsessions themselves, journalists and writers wondered what drove such people to save the peregrine. David Zimmerman attacked the question with high-psychological relish, assuming that individual endeavours to save animal species reflected a deep, personal desire for immortality. Saving a species is an 'act of immortal salvation', he explained; the 'mortal who assists in this act ... transcends his own mortal being ... here indeed is a potent human motive!'[23]

But the efforts of the Peregrine Fund and similar institutional projects could be seen as a salvation for science itself. In the new climate of the 1960s science was no longer routinely perceived as a progressive force for good, or as a disengaged, ideologically neutral intellectual pursuit. Public distrust of the scientific enterprise and its white-coated practitioners was at an all-time high. Cade and the Peregrine Fund were different. Cade was presented in the media as a heroic figure, strong, caring, passionate and deeply moral. A new breed of scientist was uncovered to a world that had lost faith in the benevolence of institutional science. And these new scientists were heroes. The Peregrine Fund became bathed in the mythical light shared by Kennedy's White House. 'In retrospect,' Cade recently wrote of those early years, 'I believe it was a kind of Camelot – a special place, at a special time, with very special people who were totally committed to restoring the Peregrine in nature.'[24]

These 'very special people' were nearly all falconers. And the thousands of years of what Cade called the 'evolved technology' of falconry provided a ready solution to the conundrum of how to release captive-bred falcons into the wild. The technique of *hacking* had been used for centuries to improve the flying skills of falcons taken as nestlings. Placed outdoors in an artificial eyrie known as a hackbox, they were fed and cared for by humans until they learned to fly and hunt like wild falcons, a process that might take many weeks, as D'Arcussia explained in the sixteenth century: 'All May and a few days of June will have passed before the youngsters have learnt their lessons and can take a perch, fly into the eye of the wind, and hang like lamps in the sky.'[25] At this point, the young falcons were trapped by the falconer and trained.

Hacking seemed the perfect solution. The only difference between conservation hacking and falconry hacking was that in the former you failed to recapture the young. Where to site artificial eyries was the next question. The urge to repopulate historic east-coast cliff eyries was strong; geographical nostalgia entwined with conservation praxis. The young would become 'imprinted'

After hatching in artificial incubators, young falcons are hand-fed with minced quail for a few days before being returned to their parents. At this early stage they're extremely delicate and need constant warmth.

on the eyrie, and thus might return once they were grown, perhaps to breed. Those who worked at the Peregrine Fund had seen falcons nesting at these very cliffs; they wanted to restore the ecological plenitude of vital local landscapes they'd seen destroyed in their own lifetimes. Hack-site attendant Tom Maechtle explained that his job gave him a deep understanding of the 'ecology of the cliff. Falcons once completed that ecology; when the falcons died, the cliffs were dead. To see young falcons flying from the old eyries is to see nature put right again.'[26]

However, the first major restocking experiments didn't go quite as planned. Without the presence of aggressive adult birds to guard the young released at historic cliff eyries, recently fledged birds were often killed by great horned owls as they slept. Five were killed in this way in 1977. 'There's not much we can do about owls except avoid them,' opined Cade.[27] Falcons hacked from eyries built on towers in untraditional sites were much more successful. Birds fledged successfully from towers in New Jersey's salt marshes, and from a 75-foot-high ex-poison-gas-shell-testing tower on Carroll Island. These highly publicized releases went well. By the early 1980s the Peregrine Fund was releasing more than 100 peregrines a year, both in the eastern US, and, with the opening of a second facility in Colorado, to much of its former range in the West. The reintroduction schemes of the Peregrine Fund and other dedicated organizations have succeeded to such an extent that the peregrine has returned to breed over much of its former American range; a landmark recovery in the history of conservation biology.

The release of these captive-bred falcons was, however, controversial. Was it right to release these birds into the wild? If the extinct east-coast *anatum* peregrines had been the last native fragments of a primeval past, what were these new birds? They had not evolved here. These were mongrel birds of mixed genetic and geographical origin, their parents hailing from as far afield as Scotland and Spain. They were not the falcons that had evolved over millennia in the eastern US. And how 'wild' were they? Surely, the distilled essence of wildness, by its very nature, should have been reared on rocks and cliffs. Is a peregrine less wild for having been incubated in forced-air machines, reared between walls?

The debates over the provenance of the released peregrines illumine deep and divisive arguments about natural value that course through conservation biology. One current in environmental philosophy values organisms or ecosystems through an appeal to their history. In this tradition, the intrinsic value of an animal or habitat is relative to the naturalness of the process by which it came to exist. No replanted prairie or rainforest is as valuable as one that naturally evolved, it contends. 'Wild' or 'untouched' ecosystems possess greater intrinsic value than those that have been affected by human activity. In this view, because they were *not* the natural inhabitants of the east-coast environment, these peregrines were a travesty; alien, 'man-made' birds. Better no peregrines than the wrong peregrines, their arguments ran.

Cade and his congeners had no truck with this attitude. Their version of nature was dynamic, inclusive, and involved deeply emotional ties to bird and landscape that supplanted naïve nativist concerns. Not only, they argued, would these new birds

A baby Peregrine Fund falcon and a crowd of fascinated Boy Scouts. Educating the public is a prime concern of the Peregrine Fund and similar organizations; A young Peregrine falcon peers from its recently opened artificial nest, or hackbox. Great horned owls and golden eagles were often a danger at natural release sites like these.

evolve to suit the new, less primeval landscapes of the east coast, but they also restored local historical and ecological continuity. Full of peregrines, the rocky cliffs and the sheer blue skies above them would once again be 'live'. Young Americans could once again watch the heart-stopping stoop of the peregrine, as much a part of the American sublime as the Grand Canyon or Delicate Arch. As Cade movingly wrote of one released tiercel,

> I tell you truly, I cannot *see* a difference with my eyes, nor do I *feel* a difference in my heart, which pounds against my chest with the same vicarious excitement when the Red Baron stoops over the New Jersey salt marshes, as it did in 1951 when I first saw this high-flying style of hunting performed by the wilderness-inhabiting peregrines of Alaska.[28]

Ultimately, Cade shows that in terms of function and aesthetics, wild and captive-bred falcons admit no difference. Genetic and taxonomic distinctions fall in the face of the animation of an entire landscape with the exhilarating flight of the falcon.

SUCCESS FOR THE FALCON?

Exuberant celebrations attended the decision to de-list the peregrine from the US Endangered Species Act in 1999. Al Gore issued an statement praising the ESA. 'Today, more than 1,300 breeding pairs of peregrine falcon [*sic*] soar the skies of 41 states,' he enthused, 'testament that we can protect and restore our environment even as we strengthen our economy and build a more liveable future.'[29] All was well; some ecological integrity had been restored; the peregrine had been saved. It was a conservation triumph. But the story is far from over. Chemical contaminants still threaten falcon populations. Researchers in Sweden, for example, find high levels of flame retardants such as polybrominated diphenyl ethers (PBDEs) in peregrine eggs. Moreover, the chemicals involved are often depressingly familiar. While legislation on pesticide use is tight across Europe and North America, agricultural chemical corporations have ready markets elsewhere. Pesticides have brought local extinction to lanner falcons in some African agricultural regions, and American peregrines that winter in South America and Mexico return to breed in the US with high DDE levels.

And full-scale ecological catastrophes still occur, though they rarely make news in the West. Mongolia is the largest stronghold of the saker falcon. There, its populations wax and wane with the population cycles of voles. Because high vole years denude steppe grassland, making life harder for nomadic herders, the

Mongolian government has recently been treating vast areas of steppe with rodenticide. In 2001 the government air-dropped poisoned grain with a concentration of the rodenticide Bromadiolone a hundred times higher than ther recommended levels. Bromadiolone is prohibited for outdoor use in the US, the country that holds the patent. A drastic decline in the populations of sakers and other Mongolian raptors has consequently occurred.

Habitat loss, too, threatens falcon populations in many countries. With the collapse of collective farming, nomadic herders no longer graze large areas of falcon habitat in Central Asia, and the resulting development of scrub and woodland on what was once grassland has reduced the populations of susliks, the saker's main mammalian prey in some regions. Mongolian sakers have

A dead saker falcon at its nest in Mongolia, killed by entanglement in artificial twine. Deaths of adult, breeding birds have a disproportionate effect on falcon populations.

also suffered from the littering of steppe grassland with non-biodegradable plastic twine and rope; many nesting sakers are killed by becoming entangled in such materials. The fall of Communism and the opening up of vast tracts of Asian steppe have also brought serious problems for Saker populations in these regions in the form of organized gangs of falcon smugglers and the attentions of local people desperate to make money from the Arab falconry market. A terrible fragmentation and reduction in the range of this species has occurred; once found from Europe right across to China, saker populations have been split into two, and both grow smaller year by year.

A growing realization of the scale of this problem has led to the creation of falcon identity databases for tracing falcon movements throughout the Gulf States; many governments there are moving toward official agreements for the biologically sustainable harvest of wild falcons. Organizations such as the Environmental Research and Wildlife Development Agency in the UAE and the National Commission for Wildlife Research Conservation and Development in Saudi Arabia have been instrumental in shaping these policies. These organizations work on other problems associated with Arab falconry, such as the traditional falcon-trapping techniques in Pakistan that exert a heavy toll on lugger falcons, used as *barak* or decoy birds to trap peregrines and sakers. And they work too on the population ecology and conservation of that most traditional quarry of Arab falconry, the houbara bustard, which is under intense pressure from falconry in much of its range.

And while it is now illegal to kill falcons in much of the world, they are still shot, trapped and poisoned. In Britain, recent peregrine declines in Scotland, Northern Ireland and north Wales have been seen as due to direct persecution. Some gamekeepers, watching their grouse stocks dwindle, see falcons as directly challenging their livelihoods. Some racing-pigeon owners living near peregrine eyries despair of the toll on their flock: to them, falcons are genuinely malevolent killers. Both are baffled by the untouchable cultural status of the falcon. After all, corvids and foxes also kill grouse and pigeons, and they can be legally controlled. Even bird protection societies destroy them on their nature reserves. What makes a falcon different from a crow or a fox? they ask. Such a question is baffling to bird conservationists whose idea of falcons as wildlife icons seems unshakeably and self-evidently true. And so conservation discourse characterizes those who call for falcon control as either misguided or evil – and dialogue between the two sides becomes almost impossible. Certainly the story is an unhappy one, and the questions it raises about the battles over ownership of the meanings of nature are troubling for policy-makers, bird-lovers and falcons alike.

A saker falcon tail-feather.

five
Military Falcons

Compare and contrast the reasons why an eagle will aggressively defend its territory with the reasons why countries defend their national borders.[1]

A TRAINED PEREGRINE stands to attention on the ARI8228 passive warning radar of a Blackburn Buccaneer. Poised on this powerful low-level British nuclear bomber, she looks ready for flight. Head haloed within the curve of the open canopy, eyes scanning the far horizon for possible targets, the bird's form irresistibly mirrors the plane – and she is a neat symbolic stand-in for the absent pilot: even her facial markings suggest a flight helmet. What is happening here? Is this merely one recent manifestation of an association between falcons and warfare that spans centuries and cultures, a snapshot resolving itself from history?

It might seem so. Russian ornithologist G. P. Dementiev described an ancient 'oriental proverb' that 'falconry is the sister of war'.[2] Eighth-century Turkic warriors were thought to become gyrfalcons after they died in combat; Genghis Khan disguised his armies as hawking parties, and fifth-century Chinese falcons carried military messages tied to their tails. And falconry trained military men as well as birds: sixteenth-century Samurai manuals had a falconry section, and falconry was a component of the

Defenders of the air: a female peregrine and a Blackburn Buccaneer.

education of the medieval European knight. Thought to foster chivalric qualities and to hone tactical skills for battle, similar virtues are still appealed to today: falconer and author Nick Fox suggests that the qualities of strategic thinking one develops as a falconer gives one the edge in – one would hope less bloody – boardroom battles. The list continues: seventeenth-century English Royalists battled Parliamentarian troops with 2 lb Falcon cannons. Three centuries later the US Air Force named their guided quarter-kiloton nuclear-armed air-to-air missile the AIM-26 Falcon. A 1946 American book catalogue described peregrine eggs as 'atomic bombs' – a heart-rendingly ironic metaphor, for those eggs were doubtless contaminated by pesticides as invisible and deadly as fallout.

But this Buccaneer falcon is not a mascot. It is a live bird recapitulating the aircraft's role, a bird literally weaponized. An integral part of British air defence systems, its task is to defend the aircraft by targeting its potential destroyers – gulls. Ever since the US built an airbase in the middle of an albatross colony on Midway Island in the 1940s, ornithology has been a branch of military science. A single bird sucked into a jet intake or flung through a canopy can destroy a plane as spectacularly as can an air-to-air missile. On Midway the US Navy hit upon radical habitat management as a solution. They paved most of the island. Albatrosses don't nest on concrete.

But the problem is not limited to the Pacific theatre: airfield grass everywhere attracts flocking birds such as starlings and gulls. Shooting them or scaring them with vehicles doesn't clear a runway and its associated airspace in seconds: but falcons do. Enter the cavalry. The falcon on the Buccaneer is from a 1970s Navy falconry unit stationed at Royal Naval Air Station Lossiemouth in Scotland. Initiated by falconer Philip Glasier, the team won its wings with a 'live-fire' demonstration to a group of officers, reporters and photographers. Clustering expectantly at the flightline, the naval officers were dubious. They were unconvinced that falcons could safely clear duty runways, and 'did not fancy having a bunch of crazy falconers let loose on their airfield'.[3] But Glasier's demonstration was flawless. Cast off at a flock of herring gulls sitting on the runway, the falcon made the gulls clear the horizon in seconds, all save for one luckless laggard she pulled from the sky.

Today, similar airfield bird-clearance units operate worldwide. The media loves their glamour; for the public they are a 'greener', more acceptable bird-control method than shotguns. And the military loves them too, for falconry units powerfully naturalize the ideology of military airpower. The unspoken argument runs as follows: if the military can demonstrate that natural falcon behaviour is the biological equivalent of tactical air warfare, then who can possibly see air warfare as wrong? It's *natural*. This

Raptors and aircraft are matched by nationality on the cover of this report. A lanner falcon and an F-16 Fighting Falcon share Jordanian airspace.

הציפורים הנודדות אינן יודעות גבולות
Migrating Birds Know No Boundaries
الطيور المهاجرة لا تعترف بالحدود

International Seminar on Birds and Flight Safety in the Middle East
Israel, April 25-29, 1999

F-4, Imperial Eagle, Turkey

F-117, Bald Eagle, USA

F-16, Griffon Vulture, Israel

F-16, Lanner Falcon, Jordan

Sponsored by:

is a crafty move, and we buy into it wholesale. If we didn't, that peregrine sitting on the Buccaneer would look incongruous. The naturalization works in part because war and nature are traditionally assumed to be utterly separate realms. 'War', wrote Karl von Clausewitz, 'is a form of *human* intercourse.'[4] But the strange history of military falcons shows, by turns bewilderingly, amusingly and horrifyingly, that the traditional supposition that war and nature are utterly separate realms is a lie.

Keep US interventionist foreign policy in mind when reading the words of a bird-clearance contractor at March Air Reserve Base, California. 'Wherever the falcons fly, that area becomes their territory,' he explained in *Citizen Airman* magazine in 1996.

'In the bird kingdom,' he continued, 'boundaries are taken very seriously. It's life or death.'[5] Troubling. For these falcons are *not* behaving territorially, of course. They are not protecting their territory from intruders. They are *hunting*. What's more, these confusions point to something about the nature of science, for the concept of bird territory itself has a military history. It was first described by British ornithologist Eliot Howard just after the First World War had decisively established the bloody realities of international territoriality on a grand scale. And in a rather less subtle naturalization of tactical air warfare in the late 1990s, the owner of the bird-clearance project at March Air Reserve Base explained earnestly that 'just as the US puts an aircraft carrier off Iraq and flies fighter sorties to establish airspace dominance, our falcons do the same thing'.[6]

But how is it the same? Is a falcon a fighter jet? Both are conceived of as pushing the outside of the envelope of physical possibility; both are often considered perfectly evolved objects in which form and function mesh so precisely that there is no room for redundancy. The falcon has long been the embodied shape of aviation's dreams of the future. Back in the 1920s, Pennsylvania falconer Morgan Berthrong recalls an aviation engineer admiring a trained peregrine above, her wings pulled back into a sharp delta shape as she glided into a stiff headwind. 'See that silhouette?' exclaimed the engineer. 'When we develop a motor strong enough, *that* will be the shape of an airplane.'[7] And yes, General Dynamics' F-16 'Fighting Falcon' was named after the bird, and there are stories that the aeronautical engineers put peregrines through their paces in wind tunnels while designing the plane. Such tales may be apocryphal, but their continuance bespeaks an urge to show the plane as a more-than-material object whose function and form are as highly evolved as that of its natural exemplar, the falcon. 'If it looks right, it flies right,' runs the test pilots' dictum. And war-bird homologies have been loaded with serious ideological weight. Kansas-based organization 'Intelligent Design' uses the plane-peregrine example to support the theory that intelligent causes are responsible for the origin of life and the universe.

MOBILIZING FALCONS

But twentieth-century falcons have been tasked with military roles far beyond airfield clearance or martial symbolism. The Second World War mobilized falcons too; and they flew for both sides. Allied planes carried a box of homing pigeons to be released if they were shot down behind enemy lines. There was a problem, however: wild English peregrines were catching and eating the pigeons after they'd crossed the Channel. Alarmed, the Air Ministry ordered that these quisling falcons on the south coast should be destroyed. Between 1940 and 1946, around 600 were shot, many eggs broken and young killed. Yet, at the same time, Allied peregrines were 'signed up'. Falconer Ronald Stevens was convinced that falcons could be used in the war – somehow. He'd heard that in 1870 trained German falcons had been used to intercept the French Pigeon Post in the siege of Paris. Stevens quickly set to work. With a friend, he built a miniature range. 'On it,' he explained, 'we put a ring of falconers round a besieged city, we covered a salient, we put a "net" of falconers behind enemy lines and in fact disposed falconers in every way we could think of.'[8] Excited by the prospects, he sent photographs of the models, along with extensive logistical analyses, to the Air Ministry.

Stevens must have been excessively persuasive, for a top-secret falcon squadron was recruited, trained and scrambled to patrol the skies above the Scilly Isles, near Keyhaven, and on the east coast between 1941 and 1943. A biological addendum to the top-secret chain of Key Home radar stations ringing the coastline, its mission was to intercept 'enemy pigeons' released from German E-boats or the like. An exclusive on the secret project later appeared in the American press. 'Operations by friendly birds were controlled just like airplanes so they knew where every bird was all of the time,' it enthusiastically explained. 'Falcons were taught to fly at great heights and to fly in circles like an aircraft on patrol duty . . . a falling trail of feathers meant another dead Nazi bird.'[9] What wasn't revealed was that the practical results of the operation were almost nil. While many pigeons were killed and one or two captured alive, only two carried messages. An RAF commander dryly related the fate of one pigeon POW – put to work 'making British pigeons' in a Ministry of Defence pigeon-loft. But successful or not, it didn't really seem to matter. The peregrines kept flying. Officers from Intelligence, the Royal Corps of Signals and the Air Force frequented the unit to watch 'thrill-ing' demonstration flights, and 'were most impressed with the hawks' performance'.[10] Of course they were. Falcons were fast, manoeuvrable, their prey outflown, out-armed and despatched with a winning 'cleanness', naturalizing the ideology of honourable combat. Falcons were a moral predator. In 1948 Frank Illingworth recalled a cliff-top peregrine-watching session. 'Mock battles are best demonstrated by two wild peregrines in playful mood,' he wrote, before continuing:

the profusion of winged movement which we watched that pre-war morning rivalled anything I saw in the same skies during the Battle of Britain . . . a few sharp wingbeats, a few chattering cries suggesting staccato machine-gun fire, and the tiercel 'fell away' like a black dive bomber ... Here were two superb fighting machines indulging in mock battle for the sheer joy of movement.[11]

In such passages, airpower evangelism meets falcon in the historical consciousness of the Romantic Right. From the dawn of the air age, a strand of thought had seen the fighter pilot as an aristocrat pitting his skill and courage in single combat with a worthy opponent, high above the messy realities of infantry and mud. Aerial combat was commonly conceived of as a throwback to an age of chivalry, the pilots as 'knights of the air'. Such dreams are beautifully articulated in the opening of Michael Powell's and Emeric Pressburger's 1944 film *A Canterbury Tale*. Powell saw the film as a crusade against materialism, a paean to English historical continuity and to the eternal nature of spiritual values. It opens with a recitation – by falconer Philip Glasier's cousin Esmond Knight – of the Prologue to *The Canterbury Tales*. Tracing a map of the medieval pilgrim's route, the screen dissolves to a scene of Chaucer's pilgrims riding along the high downland paths to Canterbury. A falconer unhoods and casts off his falcon. His upturned face is followed by footage of the falcon in flight, its flickering wings a drawn bow against the grey Kentish skies. A sharp cut that prefigures Kubrick's famous bone-to-spaceship cut in *2001: A Space Odyssey* by twenty years, and the falcon is transformed into a diving Spitfire. We return to the upturned face of the falconer – who is now a soldier watching the plane above – and instead of a line of medieval pilgrims, a military exercise crosses the downs towards Canterbury. The conflation of falcon as military aircraft with falcon as symbol of a mythical English past enabled its image to connect powerfully the idea of the nation's heritage with its recent defence through aerial battles;

'Is it a bird? Is it a plane?'
Stills from the opening
sequence of Michael
Powell and Emeric
Pressburger's 1944 film
A Canterbury Tale.

an essential, continuous national identity recoverable through the image of a bird.

While *A Canterbury Tale* attempted to show wartime Americans why they should defend Britain, in the US the weaponization of falcons was assuming bizarre forms. 'Real Warbirds for Uncle Sam', ran the headline in *American Weekly* in 1941. 'If the Time Comes When They Are Needed, the Fighting Falcon and the High-Flying Eagle May Take the Air to Put the Enemy's Homing Pigeons Out of Action.' It continued:

> While the nation's airplane factories are busy turning out bombers and fighters for Uncle Sam's growing air armada, the officers of the Army's Signal Corps . . . are thinking seriously of pressing another type of warbird into service. Known to the military mind as 'the original dive-bombers' . . . two or three hundred falcons will be trained at Fort Monmouth under direction of Lt Thomas MacClure, of the pigeon-training center.[12]

With his assistants, Privates Louis Halle and Irwin Saltz, MacClure aimed to 'reinforce the falcon's natural armament with razor-sharp knives attached to the talons, wings and body'. Not only would these trained birds be used to kill enemy carrier pigeons and take 'the dead messengers and their message to head-quarters', but 'the Army believes further that the falcons can be taught to dive at enemy parachutes and either rip them or cut the cords.'[13] He explained in the *New Yorker* that although retrieving prey to the falconer was unheard of in traditional falconry, orthodoxy was not to stand in the way of efficiency. 'War is different from falconry,' he stated firmly.[14] MacClure sent out letters soliciting donations of falcons and held a publicity talk, complete with hooded falcons, in Times Square. His rousing call did not impress one of the onlookers, falconer George Goodwin. Goodwin was the curator of mammology at the New York Museum of Natural History. He was appalled. 'If McClure [*sic*] is a sample of the Army, thank God we have a Navy!' he wrote in high dudgeon to a friend:

> Did you know that the Army has developed a method of teaching peregrines to distinguish between their own pigeons and the enemy's? Well it has but that's a Military Secret that cannot be divulged! Hallelujah! … it drives me nuts just to think of it. I'm glad to have some first hand information on the Pigeon Blitz Patrol and on McClure, but I wish to hell I hadn't seen the show they put on. I'm scared to go to sleep now for fear I'll wake up dreaming about it.[15]

Other US falconers sprang into action 'Something *must* be done,' wrote anatomy professor Robert Stabler to the chief of the US Fish and Wildlife Service. 'Can't you give this man and his group

25 U.K. Battle-Trained Falcons Will Stop Jap Fighting Pigeons

FIERCE FALCONS WILL PATROL JAP SKIES

Minsterly, Shropshire, June 5— (BUP) — A flock of 25 peregrine falcons will be sent to the Far East soon to join the war against the Japanese.

tioned on England's east coast, t falcons were sent aloft when o servers reported enemy carri pigeons approaching.

The falcons would soar to a gr height, await the enemy pige

The press seized gleefully on Lieut. Thomas MacClure's scheme to use falcons as 'real warbirds for Uncle Sam'. Here MacClure points into the sky with his right hand – perhaps he has seen an enemy pigeon?

Band of Brothers: three USAFA mascot peregrines, bound and taped to prevent injury while travelling to their new homes, have their first taste of fame.

something of an investigation? Is there no *limit* to what a man may do under the guise of defending America?'[16] And falconer and army aviator Colonel Luff Meredith took immediate steps at the War Department to ensure that MacClure's programme never got off the ground.

Meredith recruited falcons into the military in a far subtler fashion than MacClure: no Times Square event was required. He was a friend of General Harmon, who was to head the newly created US Air Force Academy in Colorado Springs. A few years after the end of the Second World War, recalled Robert Stabler, he and Meredith 'grabbed a couple of peregrines, hopped in Meredith's Jaguar' and drove down to Lowry Air Force Base; Meredith was convinced that the Air Force needed the peregrine falcon as its mascot. Harmon 'had us to lunch and we had the peregrines sitting on the back of a chair – Mrs Harmon there –

Behind the scenes, Air Force Academy personnel stare intrigued into
a box containing a new mascot falcon.

we put newspapers on the floor'. Harmon sent them over to
show the birds to General Stillwell and Colonel Heiberg; they
'picked up the birds and became immediately consumed with the
peregrine'. Stabler remembers Stillwell saying:

> 'well we will certainly present this bird as one of the things'
> . . . I think they were considering a tiger and a hawk of some
> kind and so on. 'So we'll present a peregrine and so on to
> the Cadet wings and let them vote on what they want.' And
> they did that . . . and they voted on the peregrine as being
> the mascot of the Air Force.[17]

On election day, the officer lobbying for the falcon succinctly
concluded his speech: 'the falcon has a speed in level flight of
approximately 165 mph. Its dive speed is classified information.

The golden eagle is a scavenger! You will now vote.'[18] On 5 October 1955 the first mascots duly arrived at the Academy. Held aloft for the Air Force photographer, and swaddled and bound to prevent injury en route, they look as bemused as their uniformed couriers. Since 1956 falcons have been flown at Academy football games in half-time demonstrations of airpower dominance. The USAFA website explains how falcons characterize the combat role of the US Air Force: they are fast and 'manoeuvre with ease, grace and evident enjoyment'. Courageous, fearless and aggressive, they 'fiercely defend their nest and young against intruders. They have been known to unhesitatingly attack and kill prey more than twice their size.' And of course, along with their keen eyesight, they are marked by their 'alertness, regal carriage and noble tradition'.[19] With a nod to Tom Wolfe, US military falcons are The Right Stuff.

Left to right: Chief of Staff of the US Air Force Academy Col. R. R. Gideon, Academy Superintendent Lieut. Gen. H. R. Harmon (holding 'Mach 1') and Harold Webster, falconer.

With almost inevitable logic, USAF falcons have made it to the moon. In July 1971, standing by *Apollo 15*'s Falcon landing module, Commander David Scott grasped a feather from a USAFA mascot prairie falcon called 'Hungry' in one gloved hand and a geological hammer in the other. Unrecorded by stills camera, this episode exists only as blurred video footage, a strange, charged mix of science and popular entertainment. Scott's voice breaks enthusiastically through the white noise of the lunar transmission:

> One of the reasons we got here today was because of a gentleman named Galileo a long time ago, who made a rather significant discovery about falling objects in gravity fields ... The feather happens to be appropriately a falcon feather, for our *Falcon*, and I'll drop the two here, and hopefully they'll hit the ground at the same time ...[20]

They fall in tandem to the surface of the moon. Pause. 'This proves that Mr Galileo was correct in his findings,' Scott announces. Wondrous symbolism: rather than a hammer and sickle, here is a hammer and an American falcon feather, bathed in stark sunshine through an auratic haze of lunar dust. Scott's recapitulation of a crucial experiment is broadcast as the summation of science's triumph in the conquest of space – America claiming the right to prove the laws of nature. And training a hawk can prove one's patriotism, too. 'In the final analysis,' cadet falconer Cadet Peterson explains earnestly, the US Air Force Academy's falcons 'don't have to impress us, we've got to prove to them that we are worthy of their trust.'[21]

Lying on the moon, a prairie falcon's curved flight feather and a geological hammer offer an all-American riposte to the Soviet hammer and sickle.

Fittingly for a bird so meshed with national and martial iconographies, twentieth-century falcon stories are rich with espionage. Sometimes it's merely literary: in *The Hooded Hawk Mystery*, the Hardy Boys' peregrine foils a gem-smuggling ring by slaying ruby-carrying racing pigeons. And Hasbro Toys' 2000 *Falcon Attak [sic]* Action Man comes with a natty fringed leather arm-brace and a surveilling cyber-falcon you can launch across the room. Sometimes it's real, and just as peculiar. Back in 1940 a *New York Times* headline ran: 'Hints At Goering Aim In Visiting Greenland: Ex-Air Corps Pilot Suspects A Purpose Beyond Falconry.' Below it, Captain Meredith suggested that 'now Germany has taken Denmark, considerable significance might be attached to the "falcon expedition" sent by Field Marshal Hermann Goering to Greenland in 1938'. 'To be sure,' he remarked drily,

Field Marshal Goering is, like myself, an amateur falconer, but at a time when Germany was undergoing such economic and political changes one wonders why he would go to all the trouble and expense just to get six Gyrfalcons. five members of the expedition spent almost six months in Greenland, and during that time they could not have escaped a lot of general, and perhaps specific, observations.[22]

Strange symmetries existed: Goering and Air Marshal Sir Charles Portal, commanders-in-chief of Luftwaffe and RAF respectively, were keen falconers both. So was the most infamous American spy of the 1970s, Christopher Boyce. Boyce worked at US spy satellite manufacturer TRW, where his extra-curricular activities included flying falcons in the California hills, making daiquiris in the top-secret-document shredder, and selling secret spy-satellite information to the Soviet Union under his *nom de plume* 'The Falcon'. Boyce was played by Timothy Hutton in John Schlesinger's 1985 film *The Falcon and the Snowman*. Schlesinger leans heavily on the familiar falcon symbolism, bringing the camera in to linger on the dark eyes of the peregrine as FBI agents close in to arrest Boyce: grand motifs of freedom, infinite vision and mastery of the sky.

FALCON 2020

But surely, one might ask, what about eagles? Wasn't it an eagle that Roman centurions carried on their battle standards, the eagle on the seal of the United States, or the German and Austro-Hungarian flags? Agreed: but these eagles map to nation-states, not to modern war. Eagles are large, impressive, powerful. They connote old-fashioned styles of warfare: huge armies, large-scale infantry movements and massive and deliberate strength. Falcons, however, are small. They possess immense speed, mobility and range. Falcons, not eagles, are the iconic animals of post-modern, network-centric war, built on the concepts of global vision, surveillance, rapid deployment and lightning strike. They allow a naturalization of what cultural commentator Paul Virilio describes as 'pure' weapons, weapons whose destructive capability is a function not of their massive power, but 'the rapidity and extreme precision of [their] delivery – and this as much in the sighting or surveillance of enemy movements as in the selectiveness and stealth of the strike'.[23]

In blue-sky documents such as *Joint Vision 2020* the US military dreams of future battlefields.[24] A digitized world, a seamless integration of biological units – soldiers, pilots and so on – with high technology. Military superiority is built on knowing where *everything* is, coupled with the ability to intervene in near real-time. Drenched in the terminology of complexity and air-power theory, it is a dream somewhat sullied by recent events in Iraq; winning a battle is different from strategic victory. Built on speed and omniscience, C4ISR is the preferred acronym for this metaphysical mix: Command, Control, Communications, Computers, Intelligence, Surveillance and Reconnaissance. Such is the fearsome hunger of this dream of digitized war that these military networks extend beyond the merely human and beyond the exigencies of landscape to incorporate animals too.

The idea of incorporating wild animals into military surveillance networks for conservation ends was first mooted in America in 1966 at a NASA-sponsored wildlife conference. Speakers Frank and John Craighead were no longer excited teenage falconer-photographers: they were now eminent wildlife biologists and ex-field-intelligence operatives who'd written the US Navy's Second World War survival guide. Satellites could be used to track wildlife movements, they suggested. Perhaps one could integrate wildlife-tracking data with Landsat imagery or spy-photographs from the USAF/CIA U-2 surveillance programme. Their paper was prescient.

One champion of the peregrine during the DDT years was F. Prescott Ward, a falconer and chemical and biological warfare expert who worked as an ecologist at the US Army's chemical weapons testing ground in Maryland. He helped the Peregrine Fund organize a spectacularly successful release of young peregrines from an old chemical-shell-testing gantry. Swords to ploughshares. But Ward had bigger plans: a large-scale study of the migratory habits of the tundra peregrine. These beautiful, pale, diminutive peregrines congregated on east coast beaches on their way southwards in the fall. So tame you could practically walk up and touch them, they'd been trapped by falconers for years. Falconer trappers like Alva Nye and Jim Rice knew these falcons bred in the far north, and wintered in the south. But no one knew exactly where, or the routes they took. What had been a wistful conundrum in the 1930s and '40s became an important question in the post-DDT era. For while DDT had been banned in the continental United States, it was still used further south. These migratory populations were still threatened.

And so Ward and his co-workers on the project trapped and banded migrating peregrines on the east coast; other falcon-minded researchers, like arctic specialist William Mattox, who was central in instigating the Greenland Peregrine Falcon Survey in 1972, banded falcons far further north. Others went south, hoping to spot wintering peregrines. Overall the project was as politically fascinating as it was biologically; it involved international agreements signed by the US/USSR Working Group on Wildlife, and White House staff joined the research team. But politics were no help in re-encountering banded falcons:

A satellite-tagged peregrine shortly before release.

this required luck, and the resulting migration data sets were inevitably sparse. What everyone really wanted, of course, was to capture the entire spatio-temporal pattern of a migration. So, after experimenting with falcon-mounted radiotransmitters tracked from light aircraft, the idea of miniature backpack-mounted satellite tags was mooted.

One-kilogram satellite transmitters had already been produced by the 1980s: splendid for tracking polar bears and caribou but clearly a little impractical for birds. Joint military-university research soon triumphed, however, with a new generation of miniature satellite transmitters. Known as Satellite Platform Transmitter Terminals (PTTS), they initially weighed around 200 grams – swan and goose-sized birds alone could carry them. They now weigh less than 20 grams. The PTT is mounted on the bird's back using a soft, carefully designed, temporary harness. And then the bird is released, its location determined remotely from the Doppler shift in the carrier frequency transmitted by the tag as the receiving satellite passes overhead. Service Argos, the French-operated sensor system carried on NOAA weather satellites, picks up the signals, and calculations of the bird's position are conducted at data-processing centres in France and Maryland – and the Air Force Space Command tracking facility in Colorado provides orbital elements for each satellite.

'IN GOD WE TRUST: ALL OTHERS WE MONITOR'[25]

The peregrine migration study rolled into the twenty-first century under the aegis of the US Department of Defense's 'Partners in Flight' programme, and the private/university/government partnership the Center for Conservation Research and Technology (CCRT). The Department of Defense is the third largest landowner in the US and is legally obliged to protect endangered animals on its land. Proving grounds and missile-testing ranges are not optimal habitats for roving field biologists, so remotely tracking animals by

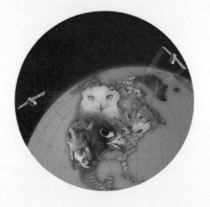

CCRT's logo
shows America
as a montage
of predatory
animal gazes.

satellite or radio is a practical solution. Yet monitoring animals in this way has ideological benefits for the US military, too. Back in the 1940s Aldo Leopold introduced the notion of the 'land mechanism' in ecology, metaphorizing ecosystems as complex engines of cogs and wheels. It was a conception of nature fitted to the discourse of technocratic militarism. CCRT biologists describe satellite-tagged peregrines as 'taste-testers' discovering 'hot spots along their route of dangerous pesticides and other threats to survival'.[26] Here the falcon is a biological probe sent out to assess the environment, a hybrid of Predator UAV and miner's canary. And satellite-tagged peregrines are more than mere monitoring instruments. CCRT biologist Tom Maechtle mused on how satellite tracking 'turns the animal into a partner with the researcher'. 'You can think of a peregrine as a biologist who has been sent out to find and sample other birds,' he explains.[27]

Maechtle's words are familiar: once again, here is a falcon biologist identifying strongly with his subject, just as the Craigheads saw their young, adventurous field-biologist selves mirrored in the eyes of the peregrine. And *Los Angeles Times* science writer Robert Lee Hotz is at pains to point out that this new kind of science doesn't threaten the old ways. Not all modern biologists stare at computer screens under fluorescent strip-lights, listening to the hum of climate control instead of birdsong. 'Despite these advanced tracking technologies,' he writes, 'the biologists ... still must catch the birds by hand.'[28] The social identity of the adventurous field biologist is unthreatened by satellite tracking. Stamina, field-craft, practical skills: these are all still required. And thus, high technology and global vision are linked with individual heroism and the soul of the wild frontier.

A heady mix. For while their conservation benefit is unarguable, the inner logic of these defence-funded tracking efforts is breathtaking. As each individuated falcon is tracked across global space, it carries far more than simply its location. CCRT calls the tagged bird a 'sentinel animal'. Each symbolically extends US technological and military dominance even as it offers myths of 'one world' environmentalism: global surveillance systems track 'American' falcons as they penetrate airspace as far south as Buenos Aires and the headwaters of the Amazon. These augmented falcons join together two incommensurable worlds – those of *military/war* and *nature/peace*. These concepts seem naturally opposed, but the satellite-tagged falcon closes the divide. The myth of falcon-as-warplane meets the myth of falcon as unparalleled symbol of wild nature, the tagged falcon a halfway house between the two systems of nature and culture, between national defence and the defence of national nature. One might see the satellite-tagged falcon as an ultimate naturalization for the military, which not only defends nature, but also promotes the notion of an ecosystem as just another complex technological system, something entirely integratable into C4ISR systems.

A new generation of bird-borne PTTS will carry advanced sensors to detect speed, temperature, humidity and atmospheric pressure, digital audio capture systems and even miniature video cameras. Sound familiar? Over the past few years, developments in US military unmanned aerial systems have produced tiny Kevlar and carbon military drones that hover or fly hundreds of feet above the battlefield, tracking military vehicles and sending live video feeds to the laptops of unit commanders. And in Idaho military training grounds, CCRT has satellite-tracked raptors in conjunction with the Deployable-Force-on-Force Instrumented Range System (DFIRST) to demonstrate the feasibility of integrating automated military tracking systems with natural resource management technology, simultaneously tracking the movement of raptors and military vehicles. The bird is tracked as an object in a system of objects. And those other objects happen to be military.

Indeed, in Alaska, the US Air Force has designated peregrine nests as surface-to-air missile sites. 'By designating known nests as simulated "threat emitter sites (areas that pilots must avoid as part of their routine training program)"', reports explain, 'the Air Force has continued realistic training while simultaneously protecting nesting peregrine falcons. This species is now recovered.'[29]

Strategic Air Command meets Animal Planet: a graphic of the travels of a satellite-tagged falcon.

The wording is highly ambiguous, suggesting that by including peregrine nests on TacAir training maps, the USAF has defended and saved the peregrine. In terms of one particular strand of falcon iconography, that might very well be true. Nature and the military achieve a discursive equality – they become symbolically equal when their positions are read through battle software, on a battle map. Defending the falcon *is* defending the nation. Attila would have been proud.

six

Urban Falcons

Even in a big city, the falcon's world is different from man's, and the two converge only at rare moments when we humans make a special effort to meet the falcon on her own terms.[1]

YOU SHARE AIRSPACE with the peregrine over London in Charles Tunnicliffe's 1923 woodcut, and its aviator's vantage too: that sense of power over, and separation from, the city below. And you and the falcon both possess that other ferociously modern ability, that of being able to set yourself against the sweep of history. Here is Roger Tory Peterson, writing in 1948:

> Man has emerged from the shadows of antiquity with a peregrine on his wrist. Its dispassionate brown eyes, more than those of any other bird, have been witness to the struggle for civilisation, from the squalid tents on the steppes of Asia thousands of years ago to the marble halls of European Kings in the seventeenth century.[2]

One of the less obvious roles of wild animals is to signify history. They can do so because they are perceived as immortal. Clearly, animals aren't immortal in the physical sense, and nor is this the animal immortality espoused by academic theoreticians, among whom at least one thinks that animals are technically immortal because they possess no language.[3] This form of immortality rests on a far more straightforward phenomenon: that a falcon is a falcon. The same falcon. Whenever it's lived, wherever it is. A fourteenth-century gyrfalcon is as indistinguishable from a modern gyrfalcon as is the peregrine photographed at its eyrie in the 1920s from the peregrine photographed there today. Civilizations rise and fall, fashions change, but feathers remain the same. And so all falcons, past, present and future, are routinely represented as if they are a single bird. A symbolic type specimen. This is the 'immortality' that gives animals an extraordinary facility for the signification of history. Like an antique vase, the falcon gains value and meaning from the hands it has passed through. Today's gyrfalcon is lauded because, in one sense, it's the same bird that Henry VIII or Genghis Khan flew, the same bird that's nested for millennia on ice-capped Arctic cliffs. And this is how Peterson's falcon partakes of what Nietzsche described as the superhistorical spirit of the modern age.

Tunnicliffe's peregrine has a name: but it is a family name; it too is immortal. For this is Chakcheck, Henry Williamson's supreme icon of aristocratic romanticism, and the hero of his 1923 nature fable *The Peregrine's Saga*, a tale far more disturbing than *Tarka the Otter*. The Chakcheck lineage is ancient, 'older than the gods of man', explains Williamson, establishing the falcon in a *longue durée* framework of essential Britishness. 'A Chakcheck surveyed the Battle of Trafalgar,' he continues. 'Another slew the Frenchman's message-pigeons before Sedan. One was in Ypres before the first bombardment.' And on he goes:

A Chakcheck was hunting the airways of the Two Rivers's estuary as the ships went over the bar to join Drake's fleet;

A peregrine falcon high over London in an illustration by Charles Tunnicliffe for Henry Williamson's *The Peregrine's Saga* (1934 edition).

centuries before, when Phoenicians first came to trade; long, long before, when moose roamed in the forest which stood where the Pebble Ridge of Westward Ho! now lies – the trees are long since gone under the sand, drowned by the sea.[4]

And this falcon is *not* at home in the city over which it flies. Williamson was convinced that urban life led to social, mental and moral decay, and the gulf between his falcon and the modern city is vast. The bird is invisible to London's inconsequential denizens who move in 'agitated streams' below. It exists in the same symbolic register as those city landmarks upon which it chooses to rest: on the cross of St Paul's Cathedral, or on another one-eyed British hero atop a column in Trafalgar Square, 'landing on the admiral's cocked hat with scratch of claws'.[5]

Williamson's peregrine is not Nietzschean solely in its historical transcendence. It is an analogue of the *Übermensch*, the 'superior man' who redeems Western civilization from its moral decadence and loss of vision. Any doubts about Williamson's political affiliations are dispelled in the virulently anti-Semitic episode in which Chakcheck is trapped by a bird-netter, an 'unshaven and insignificant individual, who worked for a maculate Yiddish "birdfancier" in Whitechapel'.[6] The netter is frightened of this warlike *Übervogel*, of course; Chakcheck attacks him, escapes, and flies back into the pure skies. *The Peregrine's Saga* clearly foreshadows Williamson's later propaganda for the British Union of Fascists.

Williamson's recruitment of the falcon as a fascist icon is a particularly distressing episode in that long-standing Romantic tradition of viewing the falcon as the spirit of a lost age – either

'Man has emerged from the shadows of antiquity with a peregrine on his wrist.' The falcon as a signifier of history: David Jones's 1948 watercolour drawing *The Lord of Venedotia*.

of vital, primeval nature, or of glorious myth and heraldry, both of which have often been held up as contrastive and ultimately normative mirrors to society and the social mores of contemporary America and Europe. Typically the falcon was viewed as the opposite of modern civilization, the scion of ageless mountains, not a citizen of modern streets. In 1942 American ornithologist Joseph Hickey wrote a scientific paper emphasizing how important 'wilderness' was to peregrines. He thought that high cliffs isolated and protected them, raising the falcons away from 'the progress of what passes for civilization below their cliffs'.[7] Like many other falcon-enthusiasts, Hickey was worried that urbanization might drive east-coast peregrines from their historic cliffs. Strange, then, that an ebullient Hickey had seen peregrines 'all over' New York City two years earlier. 'I nearly got run over by Broadway traffic 2 weeks ago watching one for *ten* minutes working an area around 72 St,' he wrote, thrilled, to a friend.[8]

SKYSCRAPER FALCONS

Yet Hickey's apparently inconsistent views on falcons and cities were not so strange. For falcons do live in towns. Lugger falcons haunt village streets in Pakistan. Black shaheens raise their young on temples in southern India. Hickey himself reported that peregrines had nested on Salisbury Cathedral in the nineteenth century. And he noted that American falcons sometimes nested on those modern cathedrals of commerce, skyscrapers.[9] Skyscrapers dominated the city skylines over which Hickey watched his falcons. Some were overtly futuristic – New York's Chrysler and Empire State buildings glittered in concrete and steel. Other high-rises reworked classical styles to extraordinary dimensions. The steel skeleton of the Kodak Eastman building in Rochester, New York, for example, was faced with terracotta and topped with a hundred-foot aluminium tower. Bettmann's photograph of Iroquois workmen on the Chrysler Building atop a eagle- or falcon-headed gargoyle projecting over the city far below is both a reminder of modernism's fascination with primitivism and a literally concretized trope of the raptor's vision and power. Atop the skyscraper, the falcon shares the cartographic view of the town planner, looking down on grids of streets and edifices of angled sheer stone and glass. As the writer David Nye explains:

> the new vista glimpsed from the upper floors of these buildings was intentional, and it quickly became an important prerequisite for executives. By the 1920s the Olympian perspective from their offices was immediately recognised as a visualisation of their power.[10]

From this height the view was sublime. It evoked the same feelings of awe and transcendence in the viewer as did views from the edge of the Grand Canyon or from Rocky Mountain peaks over vistas of wild America. But there was a crucial difference between the sublime view from a skyscraper and the view from a clifftop or mountain: from the former, the totality of civilization, not nature, was laid out below. This was a second nature, the cityscape doubling for wilderness. Mankind had proved he was indeed lord of his own creation.

Construction workers on New York's Chrysler Building in the 1940s take a cigarette break on a sublime steel perch.

But something else was sharing those views. Real falcons. They naturalized these parallels between cliff and skyscraper, nature and city. Wintering American peregrines roosted on city high-rise ledges as if they were cliffs, tail-chased pigeons hell for leather through the skyscraper canyons of Manhattan's financial district. They shared their mountain views with top-floor executives; both were high above the hustle and mess of the urban jungle below. And because these giant buildings were concrete symbols of corporate and personal power, falcons choosing to roost or nest on them had enormous symbolic import. For one of nature's most spectacular icons of vision and power had chosen *your* headquarters over those of your competitors to call home. If falcons forsook cliffs to nest on your building, you had clearly succeeded in creating an edifice as immortal as a mountain: your own Olympus. Capitalism seemed to have been granted its final approval from the falcons that chose to inhabit its most obvious symbols and whose predatory practices naturalized the aggressive competitiveness of capitalism.

The most famous city peregrines of the 1940s lived on a quite literally mountain-sized building: the headquarters of the Sun Life Assurance Company, a mind-numbingly massive edifice of pale granite rising over Montreal's Dominion Square. In 1936 a pair of peregrines 'laid claim' to the Sun Life Building, where local falcon-enthusiast George Harper Hall watched them daily. For two years, he saw the falcons nesting attempts end in disaster; the female laid eggs in drainage channels where they were soon waterlogged. And so, in 1940, Hall sought permission from the Sun Life Assurance Company to assure the future of its peregrines. He arranged for two shallow wooden boxes filled with gravel to be placed over a drainage scupper on the twentieth floor. The falcons accepted the boxes, laid eggs in one and raised two

An American peregrine, at home in city air.

young. Hall was delighted – even more so when the falcons bred again the following spring. But the company had scheduled repairs on the building's facade for May, and the falcons, busy raising their young on a diet of city pigeons, took umbrage and attacked the contractors. The workmen retreated and refused to work unless the birds were destroyed. Hall immediately took on the role of public relations representative for the falcons, and the furore over their fate was fanned not only by the local press but by the national media; letters and telephone calls poured in from across America offering advice on the matter. One young man keen to show the workmen that falcons were harmless retreated with a lacerated and bloody head, much to their satisfaction. Sun Life quietly delayed the building work, allowing the falcons to survive and the storm to subside. Everything had worked out for the best. The 'Sun Life Falcons', as they were now called, were now the most famous pair of birds in the world, their lives celebrated in articles, columns and editorials across America and overseas. Accusations flooded in that these birds were a publicity stunt: semi-domesticated birds managed by the company. 'Can the placing of a few rough boards across a water-gutter and covering them with gravel . . . be called management?' Hall retorted.

Not all peregrines were so lauded. Peregrines were still actively persecuted in this era. Some owners of New York buildings frequented by falcons actively discouraged them or destroyed their young. The rector of Riverside Church was particularly unhappy that his congregation could see peregrines killing pigeons from his church steps. In the early 1940s a pair nesting on a coping near the balcony of actress Olivia de Havilland's suite at the St Regis Hotel was bundled into a wooden box by hotel staff armed with brooms, and destroyed. Their 'dictatorial screaming' and 'preying on innocent pigeons' had upset the hotel residents – except for De Havilland, who had a penchant for falconry and was outraged by their deaths.[11] For New York falconer Vern Siefert, who exercised his trained falcons from the roof of his apartment building, the problems came from a very different quarter:

And the thing was, that the Mafia were very interested in pigeon racing. It's a funny thing . . . just loved pigeons and loved to race them. And Vernon's birds used to catch some of them, and they valued their pigeons . . . and they drove Vernon out of New York. No kidding. They scared him so he left New York. They drove him out of New York 'cause he wasn't going to give up falconry and they said, 'O.K. Really? We'll put a hit on you. We'll put a number on you.' So he came out [to Colorado].[12]

Although safe from trigger-happy sportsmen, the city was not a perfect nursery for young falcons, particularly if they fledged prematurely. There were no raccoons or foxes, but there were cats, dogs, trucks, trains, wide expanses of glass that reflected the sky and clouds and could break a falcon's neck – and a population whose response to falcons was ambivalent, to say the least. Two young falcons found by Patrolman Thomas Murphy under a car and on a building marquee in West Seventy-Third Street in June 1945 ended up in the Bronx Zoo. But the career of city peregrines wasn't ended by physical dangers like these. Their death-knell was sounded by pesticides. For despite their apparent embrace of progress, city falcons were unable to escape the chemical entailments of the consumer society. The Sun Life female ate her own eggs in 1949, and the pair disappeared from Dominion Square in 1953 after years of poor breeding performance, much to the chagrin of Sun Life, who'd commissioned Hall to write a book on their famous falcons.

However, the DDT crisis and the tireless efforts of those involved in reintroducing peregrines to the wild unexpectedly ushered in a whole new era of city falcons in the 1980s. The cultural meanings of these modern city peregrines are fascinating. Helping forge new links between corporations, governments and local communities, they have forever altered the relationship of nature and the city. And unlike their forebears, they have names.

GONE WITH THE WIND

Scarlett was the first, ushering in the era of the celebrity falcon. Though famed across the globe, the 1940s Sun Life female had no name other than that of the corporation she represented. But the 1970s ushered in a different, TV-enabled, ecologically

Scarlett, Baltimore's darling, surveys her urban domain.

aware decade. The era of the immortal falcon had ended in two important senses. First, the DDT crisis meant that the species as a whole could no longer be seen as immortal. And second, the eyass peregrines released by conservation organizations were no longer merely represented in terms of their species; they carried leg-bands that enabled them to be identified as individuals.

In spring 1979 a captive-bred peregrine that had been released two years earlier from the old gunnery tower at Maryland's Edgewood Arsenal took up residence on the 33rd floor of the US Fish and Game headquarters in Baltimore. It was a happy coincidence. She'd chosen to live on the headquarters of the very organization charged with the federal protection of the peregrine. The Peregrine Fund hacked back two potential mates for her; both disappeared. But Scarlett, as she was now named, laid three eggs, and raised captive-bred chicks that the Peregrine Fund gave her. In the following years several more tiercels, all named after characters in *Gone with the Wind*, were released for Scarlett. They helped her raise fostered chicks, for all her own eggs were infertile. She became a bona fide celebrity, a tourist draw, a media darling. She even inspired a children's book based on her life story. Finally, in 1984, Scarlett took a wild, unbanded tiercel as her mate. Beauregard, as he was called, succeeded where the others had failed: Scarlett laid fertile eggs and raised four healthy young. Tragically, as soon as her offspring were flying strongly over the Baltimore skyline, she died of a *Candida* infection. Emotional obituaries appeared in the local and national press. And the eyrie continued; a new female joined Beauregard after Scarlett's death.

Hacking back captive-bred falcons from tall buildings seemed an excellent strategy to the Peregrine Fund, Canadian Wildlife Service and similar organizations. For it solved many of the problems

A young, just-released captive-bred falcon sits beneath a CCTV camera
in Washington, DC – a particularly powerful triangulation of politics,
nature and the media.

plaguing releases on traditional cliff-sites. For one thing, there
were no great horned owls in downtown Baltimore, Washington,
Montreal or New York. And tall buildings isolated and protected
falcons from human disturbance just as the sheer cliff-faces of the
Appalachians had done decades before. But releasing falcons in
cities had an unexpected side effect: an unprecedented rise in the
number of urban falcons in North America. Everyone thought
that falcons released in cities would leave this unnatural environment to populate natural falcon habitat, settle to breed on cliffs. But
these young falcons had strongly imprinted on their 'nests' in city
landscapes, and they gravitated towards urban and industrial
sites in search of a mate or eyrie. By the late 1980s peregrines were
nesting in at least 24 North American cities and towns, and were
developing surprising and novel behaviours in their urban haunts;
some started hunting at night, for example, pulling pigeons from
ledges and rooftops in the glow of city streetlights.

The extraordinary enthusiasm of city residents for city pere-grines was also surprising. In the 1980s the US Secretary of the Interior personally approved a hacksite on the Department of the Interior Building in Washington, DC, and the Fish and Wildlife Service set up a CCTV system in the foyer showing the public live footage of the roof. In Baltimore, as well as in Washington, CCTV feeds of hacksites attracted scores of people to the foyers of falcon buildings in their lunch breaks. They were mesmerized. What was the lure of these falcons? What had brought people there?

THE SHOCK OF THE REAL

Much has been written on the disappearance of animals in the modern world. This disappearance takes many forms, most wor-ryingly in biodiversity loss and in the ever-increasing rates of species extinctions. But animals are also disappearing in other senses. One of the defining elements of the modern era is the continuing disappearance of wildlife from humanity's habitat, and by 'the reappearance of the same in humanity's reflections of itself'.[13] That is, actual animals, real live animals, have largely dis-appeared from everyday urban life. They've been replaced by images of animals shaped by the concerns of television companies, docu-mentary filmmakers, advertisers and so on. Yet the idea of animals as tokens of a deeper and more abiding reality – ironically, one that's often fostered by their media representations – has a deep hold on many people. The urge to connect or commune with wild animals seems to necessitate travel from everyday locations, everyday lives, everyday livelihoods. So, while the town or city is the setting for everyday life, the places where one can connect with wild animals are generally constrained and distant; one must go far to swim with dolphins, join nature tours, board boats to watch whales.

So deeply held are these assumptions about the correct place for wildlife in the modern world that when animals appear unexpectedly in the 'wrong' place, their impact can be immense. The office worker, for example, squinting at a computer monitor under electric light, hears a sudden thump on the window ledge a metre or so to the left of his desk. There are feathers blowing in the wind, a dead pigeon, and a falcon holding it, and he finds himself exchanging a long glance with a wild peregrine. Encounters like this have had such impact that office workers who have experienced them often speak of them in awed, religious tones, see themselves of something of an elect, singled out by the falcons for some kind of special spiritual replenishment or redemption.

Until recently, it was assumed that people were the only active participants in the urban world. Yet the presence of city peregrines on high-tech buildings and industrial spaces shows, as urban geographers have explained, that 'there is more to city living than technology and culture, or, more tellingly, more to technology and culture than human design'.[14] There is growing interest in the importance of what has been called the 'urban green' in cities. It is becoming a source of political investment for governments and authorities charged with environmental protection. People are beginning to understand how city wildlife helps to build people's civic identities. Urban peregrines, for example, create communities; their very presence can 'attach' people to their cities and to each other in strong and abiding ways. Perhaps the most heart-rendingly affective example of this comes from New York falcon biologist Christopher Nadareski, who was helping on a 'nightshift bucket brigade' at Ground Zero a few days after 9/11:

My attention turned to the sky above the 40 to 50 storeys of swirling brown smoke where I spotted a sign of survival. A pair of Peregrine Falcons circled this newly created void and landed on the observation deck of the Woolworth Building... Somehow my depression in this ravaged grave-site was temporarily overcome by the falcons displaying their solidarity with fellow New Yorkers.[15]

In New York City, as in many North American and European cities, each falcon nest is 'adopted' by people who keep constant vigil on its adults and young. Falcon pairs are often considered – always lovingly, sometimes ironically – to share the social world of their chosen nesting locale. 'Lois and Clarke live the fast-paced lifestyle of the Met Life building in midtown,' explains Nadareski, 'Red-Red and P. J. are a health-conscious couple who formerly resided at New York Presbyterian/Cornell medical centre.'[16] Actual adoption certificates for falcons are offered by the Canadian Peregrine Foundation, a charity that has for a decade been at the cutting-edge of the urban falcon

'The Shock of the Real': a female peregrine sits with her prey, an American wigeon, on an office window-ledge in Toronto.

The Canadian Peregrine Foundation offers you the chance to adopt a falcon.

phenomenon. The CPF runs a high-impact educational programme and public outreach programme on urban Canadian peregrines, and through its website offers a cornucopia of falcon data, images and stories.

Within these city falcon communities, the only people permitted to affect the falcons physically are biologists, but scientific experts are only one element in a vast assemblage of falcon-minded city people. A cadre of super-dedicated local falcon enthusiasts watch the falcons through binoculars or telescopes; they see themselves as guardians of 'their' falcons. The wider city community is involved too, as 'eyes and ears' on the ground. And perhaps the most extraordinary, and the most novel, community avidly following each nest is a virtual one. For many urban falcon nests now carry webcams that broadcast live on the web, and the communities such webcams foster are real and fascinating ones, as the next section shows.

Corporations across America have fixed upon the falcons nesting on their headquarters as symbols of their corporate environmental concern. Software giant Oracle has donated $200,000 to the University of California's Santa Cruz Predatory Bird Research Group, for example, to help fund its educational programmes, falcon website and project personnel. Falcons nested on the futuristic Oracle campus in Redwood City between 2000 and 2002 and, prompted by bird-minded staff, the 'Oracle Falcons' were given their own webcam. 'Oracle is dedicated to helping preserve and protect endangered species like the peregrine falcon,' explains Rosalie Gann, the director of Oracle Giving and Oracle Volunteers.[17]

The breeding pair of peregrines on Kodak's corporate offices in downtown Rochester, New York, are among the most famous city birds of all. And they were lured there. In 1994 Dennis Money, an environmental analyst for Rochester Gas and Electric, asked Kodak if it could put a nest box near the top of its building, 110 metres above street-level. They did so. Four years later a pair of peregrines discovered the box and bred. Perhaps we could fix a digital camera near the box to record the falcons' activities, suggested one Kodak employee. The company sprang into action, and after months of discussion with the Ontario-based Canadian Peregrine Foundation, pioneers of urban falcon webcams, they installed not only a camera, but a live image feed to a website – and the world-famous Kodak Birdcam was launched.

Birdcam is a magical phenomenon. Building on the CPF's original model, the webcam is embedded in a sophisticated website, part-educational, part-celebratory, part-product-placement

– you can buy images of the falcons from the website, via Kodak's OFOTO digital distribution service. Kodak's advice to would-be peregrine spotters in Rochester includes the line:

> Seeing these majestic birds will take your breath away, so come equipped to take lots of pictures. A telephoto lens is almost a necessity to get close pictures. The KODAK EASYSHARE DX6490 Digital Camera has a built-in 10x optical zoom lens that is ideal for taking Peregrine pictures.[18]

And just as happened with the early Canadian webcams, a diverse community of local and international 'falconeers' has been created around their shared emotional ties to the Kodak falcons. And, by extension, to the corporation itself – for visitors to the website literally see the birds through Kodak's eyes in the form

The Kodak Headquarters in Rochester, New York, home of the 'Kodak falcons'.

of four fixed-focus video cameras and a Kodak DC4800 Zoom Digital Camera. These falcons are brand celebrities: their family tree and biographies are shown on the website. And the messages left on the Birdcam discussion board are a real delight. There are poems dedicated to the falcons. There are tales of sightings, anxious enquiries about the youngsters' wellbeing, questions about falcon behaviour and habits, messages confessing that the poster has been reduced to tears by the impending departure of this year's young. There is a shared and inclusive notion of what it means to have falcon expertise. These falconeers are a sophisticated bunch; they clearly understand that in addition to showing the company's environmental commitments, Kodak's association with the falcons through Birdcam has an important branding message – and they toy with it. In a message with the subject line *Birds made me buy it*, one poster describes the 'warm feeling I now get at the very mention of Kodak . . . hate to think of what will happen when my stock broker mentions Kodak'.[19]

Many posts celebrate the guilty joy of sharing an addiction with others similarly afflicted. 'I began to post every chance I got,' wrote one regular. 'I became a "Bathrobe Brigadier" right out of the starting block. I would sit at my computer for hours at end, letting my household chores go to seed.' She continued:

During Peregrine season, we ate fast food, peanut butter sandwiches and frozen dinners. My kids loved it! None of Mom's weird veggie food to have to choke down! They were always called from whatever they were doing to come & look at the Peregrines. Sometimes, they would just get back upstairs and I would have them hurry back down to take another look. Hey, It was good exercise, running up & down those stairs! They worked off that junk food![20]

Is watching falcons on your computer monitor *really* watching falcons? Are falcon-cams simply soap operas in another guise, a nature-watching activity fit for an age of reality television? Cultural theorist Paul Virilio sees the modern world as entering an era in which 'telepresence' replaces real presence, creating virtual lives against which everyday lives become gloomy and trivial.[21] And indeed, some people criticize birdcams for promoting an impoverished experience of nature. They see it as a passive, armchair naturalism, far from the immersion in nature afforded by watching falcons at a cliff nest-site. But are these falcons virtual, unreal? Are falcon-cams just another symptom of the disappearance of animals from people's lives and their replacement with mere images, images framed by corporate symbolic investment?

Perhaps not. First, falcon-cams broadcast unscripted natural events. And although they are mediated through surveillance technology, these webcams allow you to watch and observe animals without disturbing them, in principle functioning exactly like the hides and blinds that biologists have long used to record and understand animal behaviour. Falcon-cams mean that such privileged views of natural events are no longer the province of experts alone. In Springfield, Massachusetts, the public access television channel broadcasts a live feed of a local peregrine eyrie to around 200,000 local homes. And State Fish and Wildlife Service employee Thomas French enthuses about the increase in local environmental awareness that the feed has created. 'A wildlife issue is becoming part of common conversation, not just a conversation of experts and specialists,' he explains. It's now 'part of the fabric of the city'.[22]

So webcams allow a detailed familiarity with the lives of wild animals that previously only dedicated scientists, naturalists and hunters could obtain – with difficulty. Or not at all. These live-feed webcams, then, democratize natural knowledge. As French explains, the Springfield live feed shows viewers 'the kind of stuff the professional ornithologist didn't get to see historically. People love it.'[23] And just as these webcams challenge commonly held notions of the division between lay and scientific expertise, they also challenge the notion of passive consumption of images on television and computer screens. This is where they differ from reality TV programmes. For these webcams support active agency in the viewer. Watching their televisions, Springfield's residents have actually intervened in the lives of these birds in real time. Viewers called in to say that something was wrong with one of the chicks, and French rappelled down from the skyscraper's 23rd floor to rescue the bird, which had food stuck in its throat.

Five young 'Kodak' peregrines in their technologically augmented nestbox in June 2003.

So these falcon webcams are in all senses beneficial: they create new and distinctive inclusive communities that include people and birds as active agents, both affecting and renewing each other's lives. This hybrid community is a happy one.

EVOLUTION DOES NOT HAPPEN OVERNIGHT

The world is increasingly urbanized. Natural environments are increasingly degraded by development. And birds of prey are ever more commonly inhabiting cities, using urban or industrial architecture to nest upon, hunt from, roost on. From the US to China, falcons nest on man-made structures; bridges, buildings, electricity pylons, power plants, grain silos, even the roofs of railway stations. For a long while, such phenomena seemed 'abnormal' because for centuries wild nature has been considered to exist in a realm utterly apart from that of human concerns and technology. But recently scientists have embraced the idea of the urban raptor, though not without criticism. While the Raptor Research Foundation was busily organizing a symposium on urban raptors – funded partly by power companies keen to promote their environmental credentials – there were worried questions over the ethics of holding a conference on such a topic. Would it send the wrong message to people 'more interested in economic matters than the environment and our wildlife heritage'?[24] The conference organizers were resolute in their response. There were good conservation reasons for focusing on urban raptors, they explained. Urban peregrines provide a gene pool or reservoir of birds capable of filling or refilling vacant territories in more natural environments. And importantly, they allow access to falcons that 'children and other segments of society that would otherwise never have the opportunity to see . . . in wilderness situations'. But the editors'

A pair of urban peregrines in California.

introduction to the book of the conference ends with an important note of warning:

> In these depressing times of skyrocketing human popu-
> lations, massive changes to natural environments, and
> dwindling wildlife populations on a global scale, environ-
> mentalists desperately need a positive message. This book
> offers many examples of opportunistic raptors adapting to
> human landscapes. But they cannot do it alone. [We] must
> ensure that attractive ecological features still exist in the
> environment, to help instil a tolerance in raptorial birds for
> our activities. Evolution does not happen overnight.[25]

And in June 2004 city falcons returned us once again to that ancient, robust convergence of falcons and divinity. The *New York Times* reported that peregrines were nesting on the Mormon

Hooded gyrfalcon graffiti and commuters in an underpass at London Bridge station, 2005.

headquarters in Temple Square, Salt Lake City, Utah. As the young fledged, a team of orange-vested volunteers ran around in the traffic under the nest to ensure the youngsters weren't hit by cars. 'If a bird flies into the street, Bob will try and catch it and I'm supposed to throw myself in front of the cars,' said June Ryburn, 75, a retired office manager. A couple from Washington visiting the temple with their seven children noticed the commotion. 'We thought everybody was looking at the prophet,' said McKenna Holloway, aged eighteen, referring to Gordon B. Hinkley, the president of the Church. 'Then we realized they were looking at birds.'[26]

An adult tiercel peregrine.

Timeline of the Falcon

83–72 MILLION YEARS AGO	7–8 MILLION YEARS AGO	3,500 BC	2000 BC	200 BC
Evolutionary divergence of Falconidae from Accipitrine hawks	Evolution of most present-day species of the genus *Falco*	Falcons worshipped in the Gerzean city of Nekhen, Egypt	Evidence for falconry in ancient Anatolia	Falconry practised in China

1247	1348	1486	1495	1515
Appearance of Frederick II's masterwork, *De arte venandi cum avibus*	The 59th tale in Boccacio's *Decameron* describes the fortunes of the impecunious knight Federico, who kills and serves his esteemed falcon to his lady out of love	*Boke of St Albans*, attributed to Dame Juliana Berners, is the first printed book on falconry in English	An English Act makes it illegal for anyone other than the Crown to own an English falcon on pain of imprisonment for a year and a day, a fine and forfeiture of the falcon	On the occasion of his succession to the throne, Khan Mohammed-Girei requests 'three times nine gyrfalcons, and fish teeth' (narwhal tusks) from Moscow

1860	1871	1939	1940	1960
Unconfirmed reports of peregrines nesting on St Paul's Cathedral in London	Paul Heyse contributes two controversial terms to novella theory: the 'silhouette' (concentration on one crisis) and the 'falcon' (the representation of the ethical implications of the crisis)	DDT invented	Freelance adventurer and troubleshooter 'The Gay Falcon' created by writer Michael Arlen. Played by George Sanders, he achieves cinematic fame	The first Ford Falcon rolls off the production line

AD 440	800	900	1173	1208

Attila conducts military campaigns with the *Turul* as his emblem

Falconry practised in Britain

The Laws of Wales codified by King Hywel Dda (Hywel the Good) dictate that after a good day's hawking, the king is obliged to stand to receive the lord falconer as he enters the hall

Henry II of England sends annually for young peregrines from the sea cliffs of Pembrokeshire

King John restricts falconry exclusively to the Crown

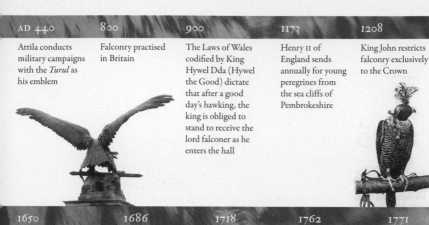

1650	1686	1718	1762	1771

Russian gyfalcon-catching cartels are granted immunity from all local taxes and duties, and have the right to receive money for food and transport wherever they travel. The falcons are transported to Moscow in a train of closed sleighs lined on the inside with felt and with mats of braided linden bark

The Duke of St Albans becomes Hereditary Grand Falconer of England at a salary of £1,500 per year

Giles Jacob explains that 'by reason of the trouble and expense', falconry is 'in great measure disused, especially since sportsmen are arriv'd to such a perfection in shooting'

Denmark imports a vast number of gyrfalcons to be sent as diplomatic presents to European states. The falcons eat 50 oxen and 20 sheep on the two-week journey from Iceland to Copenhagen

Fast-living gentleman Colonel Thornton resurrects falconry in Britain

1964	1974	1999	2000	2001

Eastern *anatum* peregrine in US becomes extinct; North American Falconers Association formed

First releases of captive-bred progeny from the Peregrine Fund. On 2 February first flight of the F-16 Fighting Falcon jet from the US Air Force Flight Test Center at Edwards Air Force Base, California

Peregrine falcon delisted from the US Endangered Species Act

Peregrines breed on Battersea Power Station in London

Massive die-off of saker falcons in Mongolia through poisoning from rodenticide-treated grain

REFERENCES

INTRODUCTION

1 W. Kenneth Richmond, *British Birds of Prey* (London, 1959), p. ix.
2 Stephen Bodio, *A Rage for Falcons* (Boulder, CO, 1984), p. 9.

I NATURAL HISTORY

1 W. Kenneth Richmond, *British Birds of Prey* (London, 1959), p. 50.
2 Quoted in J. G. Cummins, *The Hound and the Hawk: The Art of Medieval Hunting* (London, 1988), p. 190.
3 Edmund Bert, *An Approved Treatise of Hawkes and Hawking* (London, 1619), p. 19.

2 MYTHICAL FALCONS

1 Rosalie Edge, 'The Falcon in the Park', *American Falconer* (July 1942), pp. 7–8.
2 Charles Q. Turner, 'The Revival of Falconry', *Outing* (February 1898), p. 473.
3 Fable 164 from Thomas Blage, *A schole of wise Conceytes* (London, 1569), pp. 180–81.
4 Juliana Berners, *The Book of Haukyng hunting and fysshyng* [Book of St Albans] (London, 1566) [Eiv v–r].
5 Quoted in J. G. Cummins, *The Hound and the Hawk: The Art of Medieval Hunting* (London, 1988), p. 190.
6 Richard Meinertzhagen, *Pirates and Predators: The Piratical and Predatory Habits of Birds* (Edinburgh, 1959), p. 16.
7 Meinertzhagen, *Pirates and Predators*, p. 25.
8 Meinertzhagen, *Pirates and Predators*, p. 23.
9 History overview: http://www.atlantafalcons.com/history/001/051.
10 Dave Barry, 'Sex-craving Falcons Can Teach Politicians about the Hat Trick', *Gazette Telegraph, Colorado Springs* (14 July 1990), p. D3.
11 John Loft, *D'Arcussia's Falconry* (Louth, 2003), p. 261.

12 Eugene Potapov, 'The Saker Falcon', unpublished manuscript, Chapter 1.

13 Loft, *D'Arcussia's Falconry*, p. 144.

14 Three-dollar Bar Billy, speaking around 1901–2, quoted in A. L. Kroeber and E. W. Gifford, *Karok Myths* (Berkeley, CA, and London, 1980), p. 46.

15 Loft, *D'Arcussia's Falconry*, p. 143.

16 Cummins, *The Hound and the Hawk*, p. 231.

17 J. G. Cummins, '*Aqueste lance divino:* San Juan's Falconry Images', in *What's Past is Prologue: A Collection of Essays in Honor of L. J. Woodward,* ed. Salvador Bacarisse (Edinburgh, 1984), pp. 28–32.

18 Alonso Dámasco and J. M. Blecula, *Antologia de poesia española: Poesia de tipo traditional* (Madrid, 1956).

19 Quoted in Cummins, *The Hound and the Hawk,* p. 228.

20 William Bayer, *Peregrine* (New York, 1981).

21 Bayer, *Peregrine*, p. 249.

22 Ursula Le Guin, *A Wizard of Earthsea* (London, 1971), pp. 141–2.

23 Victor Canning, *The Painted Tent* (London, 1979), p. 56.

24 Canning, *Painted Tent,* p. 35.

25 T. H. White, *The Sword in the Stone* (London, 1939), p. 129.

26 White, *Sword in the Stone*, p. 126.

27 T. H. White, *The Godstone and the Blackymor* (London, 1959), p. 20.

28 J. Cleland, *Institution of a Young Noble Man* (Oxford, 1607), p. 223.

3 TRAINED FALCONS

1 Hans J. Epstein, 'The Origin and Earliest History of Falconry', *Isis*, XXXIV, 1943, p. 497.

2 Gilbert Blaine, *Falconry* (London, 1936), p. 13.

3 Blaine, *Falconry*, p. 11.

4 Harold Webster, *North American Falconry and Hunting Hawks* (Denver, CO, 1964), p. 12.

5 Webster, *North American Falconry,* p. 12.

6 Jim Weaver 'The Peregrine and Contemporary Falconry', in Tom J. Cade et al., *Peregrine Falcon Populations: Their Management and Recovery* (Boise, ID, 1988), p. 822.

7 William Somerville, *Field-Sports. A Poem. Humbly Address'd to His Royal Highness the Prince* (London, 1742), p. 7.

8 Stephen Bodio, *A Rage for Falcons* (Boulder, CO, 1984), p. 7.

9 John Gerard, *The Autobiography of a Hunted Priest*, trans. Philip Caraman (New York, 1952), p. 15.

10   Richard Barker, trans. and intro., *Bestiary* [MS Bodley 167] (London, 1992), p. 156.

11   Lord Tweedsmuir, *Always a Countryman* (London, 1953), p. 128.

12   Robin Oggins, 'Falconry and Medieval Social Status', *Mediaevalia*, XII (1989), p. 43.

13   Robert Burton, *The Anatomy of Melancholy*, ed. Holbrook Jackson (New York, 2001), II, p. 72.

14   Richard Pace, *De fructu qui ex doctrina percipitur* (Basel, 1517), quoted in Nicholas Orme, *English Schools in the Middle Ages* (London, 1973), p. 34.

15   John Loft, *D'Arcussia's Falconry* (Louth, 2003), p. 215.

16   Loft, *D'Arcussia's Falconry*, p. 267.

17   *The Art of Falconry, being the 'Arte Venandi cum Avibus' of Frederick II of Hohenstaufen*, trans. and ed. C. A. Wood and F. M. Fyfe (Stanford, CA, 1943), p. 3.

18   Marco Polo, *The Travels of Marco Polo*, ed. and trans. Ronald Latham (London, 1958), p. 144.

19   Sir John Chardin, *Travels in Persia, 1673–1677* (New York, 1988), p. 181.

20   Christian Antoine de Chamerlat, *Falconry and Art* (London, 1987), p. 171.

21   W. Coffin, 'Hawking with the Adwan Arabs', *Harper's Weekly*, 57 (15 March 1913), p. 12.

22   E. Delmé-Radcliffe, *Notes on the Falconidae used in India in Falconry* (Frampton-on-Severn, 1971), p. 11.

23   Delmé-Radcliffe, *Notes on the Falconidae*, p. 1.

24   Lt Col. E. H. Cobb, 'Hawking in the Hindu Kush', *The Falconer*, 11/5 (1952), p. 12.

25   Cobb, 'Hawking in the Hindu Kush', p. 9.

26   John Buchan, *Island of Sheep* (London, 1936), p. 26.

27   Webster, *North American Falconry*, p. 11.

28   Letter from Sig Sigwald, Collection Archives of American Falconry.

29   T. H. White, *The Goshawk* (London, 1951), p. 27.

30   White, *The Goshawk*, pp. 17–18.

31   J. Wentworth Day, *Sporting Adventure* (London, 1937), p. 205.

32   Bodio, *A Rage for Falcons*, p. 131.

33   Bodio, *A Rage for Falcons*, p. 130.

34   Aldo Leopold, 'A Man's Leisure Time', in *Round River: From the Journals of Aldo Leopard,* ed. Luna B. Leopold (New York, 1953), p. 7.

35   Nick Fox, *Understanding the Bird of Prey* (Blaine, WA, 1995), p. 345.

1 'Peregrine Chicks Hatch in London', BBC News UK edition, 8 June 2004, http://news.bbc.co.uk/1/hi/england/london/3788409.stm.

2 Dr P. C. Hatch, *Notes on the Birds of Minnesota* (Minneapolis, MN, 1892), p. 200.

3 Maarten Bijleveld, *Birds of Prey in Europe* (London, 1974), p. 5.

4 James Edmund Harting, *The Ornithology of Shakespeare* (London, 1871), p. 82.

5 Dugald Macintyre, *Memories of a Highland Gamekeeper* (London, 1954), p. 67.

6 Henry Williamson, *The Peregrine's Saga and other Wild Tales* (London, 1923), p. 222.

7 Williamson, *The Peregrine's Saga*, p. 210.

8 Ellsworth Lumley, *Save Our Hawks: We Need Them*, Emergency Conservation Committee reprint (New York, 1930s).

9 Junius Henderson, *The Practical Value of Birds* (New York, 1934), p. 198.

10 Joseph A. Hagar, quoted in Tom Cade and William Burnham, eds, *Return of the Peregrine: A North American Story of Tenacity and Teamwork* (Boise, ID, 2003), p. 4.

11 Thomas Dunlap, *Nature's Diaspora* (Cambridge, 1999), p. 255.

12 Arthur A. Allen, 'The Audubon Societies School Department: The Peregrine', *Bird Lore*, XXXV/1 (1933), pp. 60–69.

13 Frank Craighead and John Craighead, *Hawks in the Hand: Adventures in Photography and Falconry* (New York, 1939), p. 47.

14 Craighead and Craighead, *Hawks in the Hand*, p. 35.

15 H. N. Southern, 'Birds of Prey in Britain', *Geographical Magazine*, XXVII/1 (1954), pp. 39–43.

16 Southern, 'Birds of Prey in Britain', p. 43.

17 David Zimmerman, 'Death Comes to the Peregrine Falcon', *New York Times Magazine* (9 August 1970), section 6, pp. 8–9, 43.

18 Joseph J. Hickey, 'Some Recollections about Eastern North America's Peregrine Falcon Population Crash', in Tom J. Cade et al., *Peregrine Falcon Populations: Their Management and Recovery* (Boise, ID, 1988), p. 9.

19 Delphine Haley, 'Peregrine's Progress', *Defenders of Wildlife*, 51 (1976), p. 308.

20 Roy E. Disney, 'The Making of *Varda, the Peregrine Falcon*', in *Return of the Peregrine: A North American Story of Tenacity and Teamwork*, ed. Tom Cade and William Burnham (Boise, ID, 2003), p. 20.

21 Faith McNulty, 'The Falcons of Morro Rock', *New Yorker*, 23 (1972), p. 67.

22 Tom Cade, quoted in Haley, 'Peregrine's Progress', p. 308.

23 David Zimmerman, *To Save a Bird in Peril* (New York, 1975), p. 19.

24 Cade and Burnham, *Return of the Peregrine*, p. 73.

25 John Loft, *D'Arcussia's Falconry* (Louth, 2003), p. 207.

26 Tom Maechtle, quoted in *New York Times Magazine*, 22 June 1980.

27 A. Shoumantoff, 'Science Takes up Medieval Sport to Help Peregrines', *Smithsonian* (December 1978), p. 64.

28 Tom Cade, *Peregrine Fund Newsletter*, 7 (1979), p. 1.

29 A. Gore, 'Statement by Vice President Al Gore', press release (19 August 1999), The White House, office of the Vice President.

5 MILITARY FALCONS

1 'Discussion questions' Birds – animal lesson plan (grades 9–12), http://school.discovery.com/lessonplans/programs/birdsofprey.

2 G. P. Dementiev, *The Gyrfalcon* (Moscow, 1960).

3 Philip Glasier, *Falconry and Hawking* (London, 1978), p. 163.

4 Karl von Clausewitz, *On War*, trans. O. J. Matthijs Jollis (Washington, DC, 1953), p. 5.

5 Master Sgt Patrick E. Clarke, 'Bye-bye Birdies: March Looking at Adding Falcons to its Arsenal of Bird Strike Weapons', *Citizen Airman Magazine* (1996), http://www.afrc.af.mil/HQ/citamn /Dec98/falcons.htm.

6 Clarke, 'Bye-bye Birdies'.

7 Morgan Berthrong, oral history interview with S. Kent Carnie, 1990, Transcript Archives of American Falconry, p. 22.

8 Ronald Stevens, 'How Trained Hawks Were Used in the War', *The Falconer*, II/1 (1948), pp. 6–9.

9 Associated Press report, Archives of American Falconry file 86-2 (correspondence, R. Stabler, n.d.).

10 Stevens, 'How Trained Hawks Were Used in the War', p. 9.

11 Frank Illingworth, *Falcons and Falconry* (London, 1949), pp. 23–4.

12 *American Weekly,* Archives of American Falconry (n.d., *c.* 1941).

13 John E. Bierck, '"Dive-Bombing" Falcons to Play War Role under Army Program', *New York Herald Tribune* (1941), Archives of American Falconry.

14 'Falcons on Duty', *New Yorker* (30 August 1941), p. 9.

15 Letter from George Goodwin to Robert Stabler (30 August 1941), Archives of American Falconry.

16 Letter from Robert Stabler to Mr Frederick C. Lincoln, Chief, FWS,

Dept of the Interior, Washington, DC (26 August 1941), Archives of American Falconry.

17 Interview with Robert M. Stabler by J. K. Cleaver, dated 4 March 1983, Archives of American Falconry, p. 22.

18 'A Bird in Hand', *The Monitor*, XLVI/2 (March 1956), p. 16.

19 United States Air Force Fact Sheet: 'The Falcon', http://www.usafa.af.mil/pa/factsheets/falcon.htm.

20 'The Hammer and the Feather', Apollo 15 Lunar Surface Journal, http://history.nasa.gov/alsj/a15/a15.clsout3.html.

21 United States Air Force Cadet Peterson, quoted in Sam West, 'Falconry: Power, Grace and Mutual Trust', *Air Force Football Magazine* (2 October 1965), pp. 4–5, 39.

22 'Hints at Goering Aim in Visiting Greenland: Ex-Air Corps Pilot Suspects a Purpose Beyond Falconry', *New York Times* (14 April 1940), p. 41.

23 Paul Virilio, *A Landscape of Events*, trans. Julie Rose (Cambridge, MA, 2000), p. 28.

24 *Joint Vision 2020*, available at: http://www.dtic.mil/jointvision.

25 Motto of United States Air Force 5th Reconnaissance Squadron.

26 Rocky Barker, 'BSU Scientists Use Transmitters to Track Falcons', *Idaho Statesman*, reprinted in Center for Conservation Research & Technology (CCRT) *Recent Media Coverage of Field Research Efforts*.

27 Barker, 'BSU Scientists Use Transmitters to Track Falcons'.

28 Robert Lee Hotz, 'Spying on Falcons from Space', *Los Angeles Times* (14 October 1997).

29 US Department of Defense and US Fish and Wildlife Service, *Protecting Endangered Species on Military Lands* (2002), http://endangered.fws.gov/dod/ES%20on%20military%20lands.pdf.

6 URBAN FALCONS

1 Tom Cade, *Peregrine Fund Newsletter* (1980), p. 11.

2 Roger Tory Peterson, *Birds over America* (New York, 1948), p. 135.

3 Akira Lippit, *Electric Animal: Toward a Rhetoric of Wildlife* (Minneapolis, MN, 2000), p. 21.

4 Henry Williamson, *The Peregrine's Saga and other Wild Tales* (London, 1923), p. 198.

5 Williamson, *The Peregrine's Saga*, p. 211.

6 Williamson, *The Peregrine's Saga*, p. 217.

7 Joseph Hickey, 'Eastern Populations of the Duck Hawk', *Auk*, 59 (April 1942), p. 193.

8　Letter from Joseph Hickey to Walter Spofford (9 June 1940), Archives of American Falconry.

9　Hickey, 'Eastern Populations of the Duck Hawk', p. 179.

10　David E. Nye, *American Technological Sublime* (Cambridge, MA, 1994), pp. 96–7.

11　'St Regis Ejects Baby Hawks from 16th Floor Balcony Nest', *Pennsylvania Game News* (August 1943), p. 26.

12　Robert M. Stabler, interviewed by James K. Cleaver (1983), transcript, Archives of American Falconry, p. 33.

13　Lippit, *Electric Animal*, p. 25.

14　Steve Hinchcliffe and Sarah Whatmore, 'Living Cities: Towards a Politics of Conviviality', *Science as Culture*, XV/2, special issue on technonatures (2006).

15　Tom Cade and William Burnham, eds, *Return of the Peregrine: A North American Story of Tenacity and Teamwork* (Boise, ID, 2003), p. 99.

16　Cade and Burnham, *Return of the Peregrine*, p. 99.

17　University of California Santa Cruz press release (19 January 2005).

18　'Visiting the Falcon's Neighborhood', http://www.kodak.com/eknec/ PageQuerier.jhtml?pq-path=38/492/2017/2037/2063&pq-locale= en_US.

19　Karen Gus, Kodak Birdcam discussion board, 07:57am 18 July 2003 EST (#17821 of 17889).

20　Hootie, Kodak Birdcam discussion board, 09:14pm 17 July 2003 EST (#17763 of 17889).

21　P. Virilio, 'The Visual Crash', in *Rhetorics of Surveillance from Bentham to Big Brother,* ed. T. Y. Levin, U. Frohne and P. Weibel (Karlsruhe, 2002), p. 109.

22　Quoted in Doreen Leggett, 'Peregrine Falcons', *Cape Codder* (28 January 2005), http://ww2.townonline.com/brewster/local Regional/view.bg?articleid=174563.

23　Legget, 'Peregrine Falcons'.

24　D. Bird, D. Varland and J. Negro, eds, *Raptors in Human Landscapes* (London, 1996), p. xvii.

25　Bird, Varland and Negro, *Raptors in Human Landscapes*, p. xviii.

26　Melissa Sanford, 'For Falcons as for People, Life in the Big City has its Risks as Well as its Rewards', *New York Times* (28 June 2004), section A, p. 12, col. 1.

BIBLIOGRAPHY

Anderson, S. H., and J. R. Squires, *The Prairie Falcon* (Austin, TX, 1997)

Baker, John Alec, *The Peregrine* (New York, 2005)

Blaine, Gilbert, *Falconry* (London, 1936)

Bodio, Stephen, *A Rage for Falcons* (Boulder, CO, 1984)

Burnham, William, *A Fascination with Falcons: A Biologist's Adventures from Greenland to the Tropics* (Blaine, WA, 1997)

Cade, Tom, and William Burnham, eds, *Return of the Peregrine: A North American Saga of Tenacity and Teamwork* (Boise, ID, 2004)

Chamerlat, Christian Antoine de, *Falconry and Art* (London, 1987)

Craighead, Frank, and John Craighead, *Hawks in the Hand: Adventures in Photography and Falconry* (Boston, MA, 1939)

—, *Life with an Indian Prince* (Boise, ID, 2001)

Craighead George, Jean, *My Side of the Mountain* (New York, 1959)

Cummins, John, *The Hound and the Hawk: The Art of Medieval Hunting* (London, 1988)

Enderson, Jim, *Peregrine Falcon: Stories of the Blue Meanie* (Austin, TX, 2005)

Ford, Emma, *Gyrfalcon* (London, 1999)

Fox, Nick, *Understanding the Bird of Prey* (Blaine, WA, 1994)

Frederick II of Hohenstaufen, *The Art of Falconry, being the 'Arte Venandi cum Avibus' of Frederick II of Hohenstaufen*, trans. and ed. C. A. Wood and F. M. Fyfe (Stanford, CA, 1943)

Fuertes, Louis Agassiz, 'Falconry, the Sport of Kings', *National Geographic*, XXXVIII/6 (1922), pp. 429–60

Glasier, Philip, *As the Falcon Her Bells* (London, 1963)

—, *Falconry and Hawking* (London, 1978)

Haak, Bruce, *Pirate of the Plains: The Biology of the Prairie Falcon* (Blaine, WA, 1995)

Loft, John, trans. and ed., *D'Arcussia's Falconry* (Louth, Lincs, 2003)

Oggins, Robin S., *The Kings and their Hawks: Falconry in Medieval England* (New Haven, CT, 2004)

Parry-Jones, Jemima, *Jemima Parry-Jones' Falconry: Care, Captive Breeding and Conservation* (Newton Abbot, 1993)

Potapov, Eugene, and Richard Sale, *The Gyrfalcon* (London, 2005)

Ratcliffe, Derek, *The Peregrine* (London, 1980)

Tennant, Alan, *On the Wing: To the Edge of the Earth with the Peregrine Falcon* (New York, 2004)

Treleaven, R. B., *In Pursuit of the Peregrine* (Wheathampsted, Herts, 1998)

Upton, Roger, *A Bird in the Hand: Celebrated Falconers of the Past* (London, 1980)

——, *Arab Falconry: History of a Way of Life* (Blaine, WA, 2001)

Zimmerman, David, *To Save a Bird in Peril* (New York, 1975)

ASSOCIATIONS AND WEBSITES

ARCHIVES OF FALCONRY
www.peregrinefund.org/american_falconry.asp

BRITISH FALCONERS CLUB
www.britishfalconersclub.co.uk

BRITISH TRUST FOR ORNITHOLOGY
www.bto.org

CANADIAN PEREGRINE FOUNDATION
www.peregrine-foundation.ca

EMIRATES FALCONERS CLUB
www.emiratesfalconersclub.com

HAWK AND OWL TRUST
www.hawkandowl.org

HAWKWATCH INTERNATIONAL
www.hawkwatch.org

INTERNATIONAL ASSOCIATION FOR FALCONRY & BIRDS OF PREY
www.i-a-f.org

INTERNATIONAL CENTER FOR BIRDS OF PREY
www.internationalbirdsofprey.org

INTERNATIONAL FALCONER MAGAZINE
www.intfalconer.com

KODAK BIRDCAM
birdcam.kodak.com

MARSHALL RADIO TELEMETRY
www.marshallradio.com

MARTIN JONES FALCONRY EQUIPMENT
www.falconryonline.com

NORTH AMERICAN FALCONERS' ASSOCIATION
www.n-a-f-a.org

NORTHWOODS FALCONRY EQUIPMENT
www.northwoodsfalconry.com

THE PEREGRINE FUND
www.peregrinefund.org

RAPTOR RESEARCH CENTER
http://rrc.boisestate.edu

RAPTOR RESEARCH FOUNDATION
http://biology.boisestate.edu/raptor

SANTA CRUZ PREDATORY BIRD RESEARCH GROUP
www2.ucsc.edu/scpbrg

SAVE THE SAKER
www.savethesaker.com

WINGSPAN BIRD OF PREY TRUST, NEW ZEALAND
www.wingspan.co.nz

WORLD WORKING GROUP ON BIRDS OF PREY AND OWLS
www.raptors-international.de

ACKNOWLEDGEMENTS

My thanks to Jonathan Burt, Michael Leaman, Harry Gilonis, and to friends and colleagues who supplied photographs and images and commented on the manuscript: Stephen Bodio, Tom Cade, Erin Gott, Nick Jardine, Rob Jenks, John Loft, James Macdonald, Tamsin Mather, Rob Ralley, Mark Sprevak, Roy Wilkinson and Charles Young. Special thanks are due to Colonel S. Kent Carnie, Archivist of the Archives of Falconry in Boise, Idaho, for his wonderful hospitality and assistance to an expat researcher; to Nick Fox, who generously allowed use of his photographic archives; and to Eugene Potapov for information on falcon myths in Central Asia. The financial assistance of Jesus College, Cambridge, and the Williamson Fund of the Department of History and Philosophy of Science, University of Cambridge, helped with picture reproductions. I am hugely grateful to Christina McLeish for support throughout the writing up of the manuscript. And last of all, very special thanks are due to my infinitely patient parents, who let a small girl's kestrel roost at night on her bedroom bookcase, despite the mess.

PHOTO ACKNOWLEDGEMENTS

The author and publishers wish to express their thanks to the below sources of illustrative material and/or permission to reproduce it. Some sources uncredited in the captions for reasons of brevity are also given below. We would appreciate hearing from any copyright holder whom we have been unable to trace.

Images © Shujaat Ali/Al Jazeera: pp. 116; from *Animal World*, vol. xx, no. 237 (June 1889): p. 115; courtesy of the Archives of Falconry (formerly Archives of American Falconry): pp. 57 (top), 71, 80, 92, 113, 125, 129 (photo Charles E. Proctor), 158, 159, 160, 161; courtesy of the author: pp. 24, 147, 200–201; photo © Bettmann/Corbis: p. 179; Biblioteca Civica, Padua: p. 98; The British Council: p. 177; by permission of the British Library, London: pp. 22 (from an album of *c.* 1802, 'The Natural Products of Hindostan', MS NHD 7/1010), 53 (from Peter de Langtoft, *Chronicle of England*, MS Royal 20 A. ii, f.7); from Montagu Browne, *Practical Taxidermy: A Manual of Instruction to the Amateur* . . . (London, 1884): p. 122; photo courtesy of the Canadian Peregrine Foundation: p. 190; courtesy of the Center for Conservation Research and Technology, Baltimore: pp. 167, 168, 171; photo by Chas E. Clifton, courtesy The Peregrine Fund: p. 143 (right); photo by Glen Eitemiller, courtesy The Peregrine Fund: p. 138; courtesy of the Environmental Research and Wildlife Development Agency (EWRDA): p. 36; after Nick Fox, *Understanding the Bird of Prey* (Surrey, BC, 1995): p. 37; photo by Nick Fox, courtesy of International Wildlife Consultants, p. 89; photo courtesy of the Freud Museum, London: p. 60; photo by Erin Gott, courtesy of The Peregrine Fund, p. 17; photo by Noel Hyde: p. 29; photo © Norman Kent, courtesy of Norman Kent Productions and Ken Franklin: p. 14; photos courtesy of Eastman Kodak Company: pp. 192, 195; photo courtesy of the Kunsthistoriches Museum, Vienna: p. 99; Gyula László: p. 63; photos courtesy of the Library of Congress, Washington, DC (Prints and Photographs Division): pp. 108 (G. Eric and Edith Matson Photograph Collection, LC-M36-630), 200 [bottom left] (LC-DIG-ppmsc-08571); photo © James Macdonald: p. 198; photo by Tom Maechtle, courtesy The Peregrine Fund: p. 184; Musée d'Histoire Naturelle,

INDEX